NATIONAL SECURITY RESEARCH DIVISION

H4CKER5 WANTED

An Examination of the Cybersecurity Labor Market

MARTIN C. LIBICKI
DAVID SENTY
JULIA POLLAK

This research was sponsored by a private foundation and conducted within the Forces and Resources Policy Center of the RAND National Security Research Division (NSRD). NSRD conducts research and analysis on defense and national security topics for the U.S. and allied defense, foreign policy, homeland security, and intelligence communities and foundations and other nongovernmental organizations that support defense and national security analysis.

Library of Congress Cataloging-in-Publication Data is available for this publication.

ISBN: 978-0-8330-8500-9

Preface

There is general agreement that jobs for cybersecurity professionals are going unfilled within the United States (and the world), particularly within the federal government, notably those working on national and homeland security as well as intelligence. Such unfilled positions complicate securing the nation's networks and may leave the United States ill-prepared to carry out conflict in cyberspace. RAND undertook to understand the nature and source of this challenge, how national security entities (including the private sector) are responding to labor market conditions, the policies that have been implemented or referenced to help increase the supply of cybersecurity professionals, and the requirement for further policies as needed to meet the needs of the national security establishment.

This research was sponsored by a private foundation and conducted within the Forces and Resources Policy Center of the RAND National Security Research Division (NSRD). NSRD conducts research and analysis on defense and national security topics for the U.S. and allied defense, foreign policy, homeland security, and intelligence communities and foundations and other nongovernmental organizations that support defense and national security analysis.

For more information on the RAND Forces and Resources Policy Center, see http://www.rand.org/nsrd/ndri/centers/frp.html or contact the director (contact information is provided on the web page).

Contents

Figures and Table

Figures

Table

Summary

There is a general perception that there is a shortage of cybersecurity professionals within the United States (indeed, in the world), and a particular shortage of these professionals within the federal government, notably those working on national and homeland security as well as intelligence. Shortages of this nature complicate securing the nation's networks and may leave the United States ill-prepared to carry out conflict in cyberspace.

In response, RAND undertook to examine the current status of the labor market for cybersecurity professionals—with an emphasis on their being employed to defend the United States. We carried out this effort in three parts: first, a review of the literature; second, a set of semi-structured interviews with managers and educators of cybersecurity professionals, supplemented by reportage as appropriate; and third, an examination of what the economic literature suggests about labor markets for cybersecurity professionals. RAND also looked within the broad definition of "cybersecurity professionals" to unearth skills differentiation as relevant to this study.

Literature

There have been several excellent reports on the difficulty of meeting cybersecurity manpower needs; those by Booz Allen Hamilton, the Center for Strategic and International Studies, and the Department of Homeland Security's Homeland Security Advisory Council have been among the most comprehensive. Their underlying message is the same:

A shortage exists, it is worst for the federal government, and it potentially undermines the nation's cybersecurity. Such reports mention the many steps that the government has already taken to increase security, notably the establishment of scholarships, the more sophisticated definition of skill requirements, and the encouragement of hacker competitions (to publicize the field, motivate those looking for careers, and prescreen for talented individuals). All of these reports recommend more careful and painstaking management of the supply-demand balance for cybersecurity workers. None of them recommends steps to reduce the demand for such individuals.

Interviews et al.

We carried out semi-structured interviews with representatives of five U.S. government organizations, five education institutions, two security companies, one defense firm, and one outside expert. Our key findings follow.

- The cybersecurity manpower shortage—more accurately, the rising difficulty of finding and retaining qualified individuals at what are considered reasonable wages—is predominantly at the high end of the capability scale: roughly the top 1–5 percent of the overall workforce. These are the people capable of detecting the presence of advanced persistent threats, or, conversely, finding the hidden vulnerabilities in software and systems that allow advanced persistent threats to take hold of targeted systems. Such individuals can often claim compensation above $200,000–$250,000 a year—although capturing such salaries requires a mix of talents and soft skills (e.g., marketing, management), which means recipients are far more likely to be in their 30s than in their 20s (a factor which also extends the lead time required to get new people into such positions).
- The larger organizations—both private and public—have found ways of coping with tightening labor markets, in large part through internal promotion and education, a route that is less

attractive to smaller organizations that (rightly) fear that those they expensively educate will take their training to other employers. The larger defense contractors have a marked advantage in that most of their professional labor force is already technically trained, and thus some percentage of them will have a discoverable talent for cybersecurity work. Large organizations (e.g., the Air Force) have the scope to define internal specializations that allow them to train individuals intensely (albeit narrowly) to meet such task requirements.

- In recent years, organizations have become increasingly sophisticated in defining those personality characteristics that correlate well with cybersecurity requirements, notably an intense curiosity with how things work (and can be made to fail). This has allowed such organizations to promote and train more effectively from within without having to wait for such individuals to graduate with specialized degrees.
- Universities have risen to the challenge of training cybersecurity specialists. In the last few years there has been some growth in programs, and definitely more students in existing programs. Finding qualified professors does not seem to have been a problem. Part of the reason is that the demand for information technology is down from peaks reached circa 2000 at the height of the dot-com era, leaving considerable institutional spare capacity, so to speak. Universities have also done a credible job finding individual niches to explore: among those we interviewed one specializes in industrial control systems, another in applications at scale, a third in cybersecurity management, and a fourth in cybersecurity public policy.

Economics

We examined whether the literature on labor and personnel economics can shed light on recent developments in the market for cybersecurity professionals. Consistent with economic theory, we find that the rapid rise in the demand for cybersecurity professionals has been accompanied by a sharp rise in compensation packages. The reason is that in the short run, the supply of cybersecurity professionals is fairly unresponsive to higher compensation—it takes time to train additional workers with the required skills. In the longer run, economic theory suggests that today's higher compensation will attract newcomers to the field. Thus, supply should increase, and the growth in compensation packages should decelerate, although compensation will likely remain above its 2007 level.

There are a variety of factors that complicate this simplified view of the labor market for cybersecurity professionals. First, demand as well as supply may take time to react to an increased awareness about cybersecurity. Although demand for cybersecurity personnel rose following the 2007 cyberattacks on Estonia and revelations about Chinese intrusions into the Department of Defense (DoD), some employers may have been reluctant to increase hiring immediately because of costs associated with hiring or firing workers. Second, there are important differences across cybersecurity professionals in terms of human capital. According to our interviews, upper-tier cybersecurity professionals—those who are qualified to do forensics, code-writing, or red-teaming—are the hardest to hire in today's labor market. Compounding this challenge is the particular difficulty of identifying a potential employee's talent for these tasks. Organizations have, thus, developed a variety of ways to screen for potential talent, including traditional methods such as written applications and interviews, as well as unconventional methods such as hackathon participation. Third, government agencies face additional challenges, above and beyond those faced by private-sector firms, in hiring cybersecurity professionals. Perhaps most important are employee pay bands, which are most likely to be binding for upper-tier professionals. Thus, government employers may find it difficult to hire enough upper-tier professionals, even when the private sector does not. One way to address this challenge—which we observed in our interviews—is for agencies to focus on hiring entry-level workers, and to provide substantial training.

Policy Options

We looked at several major policy options that have been adduced to address the tight market in cybersecurity manpower.

- One is to use more foreign nationals, notably by making it easier for those with advanced degrees to stay and work in the United States. Despite the general merit of such ideas, it is easy to exaggerate how much this would help. Many such individuals (ironically, particularly from China) already find ways to stay here, a large share of cybersecurity work can be carried out overseas (e.g., bug-hunting), and requirements for U.S. citizenship limit the help that increasing the number of such individuals would provide to meeting national security needs.
- A proposal to develop an intensive two-year (junior college) program in cybersecurity appears problematic. Those with the talent to be upper-tier cybersecurity professionals (who are said to be the hardest to hire in today's market) are unlikely to be satisfied with an associate's degree. Such education also produces a corps of intensively educated individuals that would be difficult to employ if the requirements for cybersecurity work change substantially—as they surely will, given the volatility of the field.
- Many individuals have lauded the work going into differentiating job categories more precisely. Despite its value for task planning, such an effort is unlikely to make so much difference in matching cybersecurity manpower requirements and personnel, because the match between how people are educated and what jobs they are good at is not that tight.
- Addressing civil service and veterans preferences issues is always conducive to a better supply-demand match within civilian federal employment, but there is no particular reason to believe that its benefits are specific to cybersecurity (except that the federal government is hiring cybersecurity experts at a time when it is cutting back on other specialties).
- Using Guard and Reserve units would, again, help, but not across the board. Unfortunately for most cybersecurity tasks (foren-

sics conspicuously aside), effective cybersecurity defense requires familiarity with the systems being attacked—something that part-time exposure does not provide very well (although such units can re-create communications infrastructure using technologies such as very small-aperture satellite terminals under auspices of Defense Support to Civil Authorities).

- One route that gets little attention is reducing the demand for cybersecurity professionals by finding other ways to reduce cyber-security issues. Local options include limiting the use of problem-atic applications (e.g., Java); global options include encouraging the proliferation of harder or at least more closed systems (e.g., iOS). Moreover, there is a growing high-level initiative to "fix the architecture" of personal computers and the networks they sit on.

Recommendations

In the course of our work, we came across potential ideas whose costs were modest but which could appreciably help find good cybersecurity professionals. They include more active waiving of civil service rules that impede hiring talented cybersecurity professionals, maintaining government hiring of cybersecurity professionals even through adverse events such as sequestrations, funding software licenses and related equipment for educational programs, refining tests to identify candi-dates likely to succeed in cybersecurity careers, and, in the longer run, developing methods to attract women into the cybersecurity profession.

But, in general, we support the use of market forces (and preex-isting government programs) to address the strong demand for cyber-security professionals in the longer run. Prior to 2007 (marked by the cyberattacks on Estonia and revelations about Chinese intrusions into DoD), there was little urgency for improving cybersecurity. The first official recognition of the need was the 2008 Comprehensive National Cybersecurity Initiative. Initiatives undertaken or accelerated at that point are just now reaching fruition. The increase in education and training opportunities, coupled with the increase in compensation packages, will draw more workers into the profession over time. Cybersecurity professionals take time to reach their potential, anyway. Drastic steps taken today to increase their quantity and quality would not bear fruit for another five to ten years. By then, the current concern over cybersecurity may prove prescient but could alternatively as easily abate, driven by new technology and more secure architecture. Pushing too many people into the profession now could leave an overabundance of highly trained and narrowly skilled individuals who could better be serving national needs in other vocations.

Acknowledgments

We wish to gratefully acknowledge Ryan Henry and Steve Kistler at RAND, who helped with the early conceptualization of this project.

Among those who helped in creating this document, we wish to acknowledge Rena Rudavsky and Barbara Bicksler, who supplied some of the early research, Francisco Perez-Arce, who supplied some of the later research, and Francisco Walter, who helped manage the paperwork. We are grateful for the many individuals working in government, industry, and academia who lent us their time to answer our inquiries.

Finally, we wish to acknowledge the careful work and guidance that we received from our reviewers Sasha Romanosky and Nathan Wozny as well as from Shanthi Nataraj and John Winkler, who helped shepherd this manuscript through the quality assurance process.

Abbreviations

ACM	Association for Computing Machinery
AFSC	Air Force Specialty Code
APT	advanced persistent threat
BAH	Booz-Allen Hamilton (original name)
CAE	Centers of Academic Excellence
CEO	Chief Executive Officer
CIA	Central Intelligence Agency
CIO	Chief Information Officer
CISO	Chief Information Security Officer
CISSP	certified information system security professional
CNCI	Comprehensive National Cybersecurity Initiative
CONOPS	concept of operations
CRA	Computing Research Association
CREST	Council of Registered Ethical Security Testers
CSIS	Center for Strategic and International Studies
DEF CON	an annual hacker conference
DHS	Department of Homeland Security
DISA	Defense Information Systems Agency

DLAT	Defense Language Aptitude Test
DoD	Department of Defense
DoDIN	DoD Information Network
EOD	explosive ordnance disposal
FBI	Federal Bureau of Investigation
FCIP	Federal Career Intern Program
GAO	U.S. Government Accountability Office
GS	General Service
HR	human resources
IASP	Information Assurance Scholarship Program
ICT	information-communications technology
IEEE	Institute for Electrical and Electronic Engineering
INSCOM	U.S. Army Intelligence and Security Command
iOS	the operating system for Apple's iPhone
IPA	Intergovernment Personnel Act
ISACA	Information Systems Audit and Control Association
IT	information technology
JIE	Joint Information Environment
JTF-GNO	Joint Task Force Global Network Operations
NASA	National Aeronautics and Space Administration
NATO	North Atlantic Treaty Organization
NDU	National Defense University
NICE	National Initiative for Cybersecurity Education
NIST	National Institute of Standards and Technology
NSA	National Security Agency
NSF	National Science Foundation

OMB	Office of Management and Budget
OPM	Office of Personnel Management
OPT	Optional Practical Training
PDF	portable document format
SANS Institute	An organization specializing in cybersecurity education
SFS	Scholarship-for-Service
STEM	science, technology, engineering, and mathematics
USAF	U.S. Air Force
USCYBERCOM	U.S. Cyber Command
USNA	U.S. Naval Academy

Prologue

Within the last five years there has been a widespread drumbeat of concern about the perceived difficulty of finding qualified people to defend the nation's networks, currently under assault by terrorists, spies, and criminals.

According to a 2010 story on NPR, "There may be no country on the planet more vulnerable to a massive cyberattack than the United States, where financial, transportation, telecommunications and even military operations are now deeply dependent on data networking. U.S. industry, government and military operations are all at risk of an attack on complex computer systems, analysts warn. What's worse: U.S. security officials say the country's cyberdefenses are not up to the challenge. In part, it's due to having too few computer security specialists and engineers with the skills and knowledge necessary to do battle against would-be adversaries. The protection of U.S. computer systems essentially requires an army of cyberwarriors, but the recruitment of that force is suffering" (Gjelten, 2010).

As bad as matters are for well-heeled employers, the problem may be more severe for the federal government, said to lack the people to defend the networks that help defend the nation. In 2009, *Washington Post* reported, "The federal government is struggling to fill a growing demand for skilled computer-security workers, from technicians to policymakers, at a time when network attacks are rising in frequency and sophistication. Demand is so intense that it has sparked a bidding war among agencies and contractors for a small pool of 'special' talent: skilled technicians with security clearances. Their scarcity is driving up

1

salaries, depriving agencies of skills, and in some cases affecting project quality, industry officials said." It further cited an employee who won a 45 percent raise by jumping from the NSA to a major contractor, and a further raise by jumping to a small employer who observed, "The pay difference is so dramatic now, you can't ignore it." Another *Post* source, a military officer with 20 years' cybersecurity experience and a coveted security clearance, was overwhelmed: "It's mind-roasting. . . . I've had people call my house, recruiters for defense contractors . . . probably 20 calls" (Nakashima and Krebs, 2009).

Last May, *Bloomberg News* quoted Diane Miller, Northrop's program director for the CyberPatriot contest, who said "We just have a shortage of people applying" for 700 currently open positions. This observation was echoed by Ryan Walters, who founded mobile data security company TerraWi Inc. in 2009: "I cannot hire enough cybersecurity professionals, I can't find them, they're not qualified." His 12-person firm was planning to expand to 20; the article went on to note, "Listings for cybersecurity positions rose 73 percent in the five years through 2012, 3.5 times faster than postings for computer jobs as a whole, according to Boston-based Burning Glass, a labor market analytics firm that collects data from more than 22,000 online jobs sites." Alan Paller, CEO of SANS, a cybersecurity-education organization, told Bloomberg "We have a huge number of frequent flyers and a tiny number of fighter pilots." Finally, the story cited a letter written by JPMorgan Chase's CEO saying that the bank "spends approximately $200 million to protect ourselves from cyberwarfare and to make sure our data are safe and secure [with 600 people dedicated to the task]. . . . This number will grow dramatically over the next three years" (Rastello and Smialek 2013).

Those who are qualified are spoiled for choices: "Pretty much everyone here at the conference could quit their jobs and have another job by the end of the day," said Gunter Ollmann, vice president of research at Damballa, an Atlanta-based security firm focused on cyberthreats and other remotely controlled criminal threats. "The number of security companies is growing" (Brannigan, 2012).

In mid-2012, Jeff Moss, a prominent hacking expert who sits on the Department of Homeland Security Advisory Council, told a

Reuters conference, "None of the projections look positive. . . . The numbers I've seen look like shortages in the 20,000s to 40,000s for years to come." A study earlier this year by the industry group (ISC)² found that 83 percent of federal hiring managers surveyed said it was extremely difficult to find and hire qualified candidates for cybersecurity jobs (Lord and Stokes, 2012).

These are serious statements of concern. But is what is commonly referred to as a shortage of cybersecurity professionals a long-term crisis or a short-term problem? Is it pervasive throughout the sector or in certain segments within the sector? What potential policy options exist for addressing these concerns? Our report addresses these questions.

Organization

The remainder of this report will explore the cybersecurity manpower problem by teasing it apart into its components.

Chapter One lays out the cybersecurity manpower problem. It does so in the aggregate and then disaggregates the problem by type of employer and skill class.

Chapter Two surveys the existing literature on the specific topic of cybersecurity manpower. By literature, we primarily mean the policy reports that have taken, as their driving assumption, the existence of a shortage and have examined various options for resolving it. By doing so, we not only illustrate how the cybersecurity community is thinking about the issue, but, because many reports highlight as much, show what the government is already doing about it.

Chapter Three is built upon a set of semi-structured interviews, although its observations and arguments also include material such as new reports. We interviewed a mix of educators and representatives of large organizations to gather their perspectives on how to cope with the current difficulties in the market and what policies to pursue to stabilize the market in the long run.

Chapter Four presents foundational material on labor and personnel economics, with a view to understanding the labor market for cybersecurity professionals. It is broadly recognized that the demand for cybersecurity professionals has risen sharply in recent years, notably since 2007 (when Russian hackers attacked Estonia, and cyberespionage from China acquired a public reputation for its pervasiveness). We examine how economic theory predicts the labor market for cybersecurity professionals will react to this increase in demand, including how government agencies (in contrast with private-sector firms) are likely to be affected.

In Chapter Five, we first discuss in detail the distinction between markets for upper-tier cybersecurity professionals and for the rest. The latter half of the chapter frames a number of policy questions for alleviating the (notably federal) difficulties in accessing labor market professionals (e.g., federal hiring practices).

Chapter Six concludes by examining potential policy options, including the all-important option of doing nothing or, more specifically (because the government is doing quite a lot to address its issues with the market for cybersecurity professionals), doing nothing further.

CHAPTER ONE

Why Has Demand Risen Sharply?

When demand rises sharply and supply is relatively unresponsive, the result is usually higher prices. In markets where prices are constrained—for example, the market for oil in the 1970s—shortages are another consequence. Within the last five years, the demand for cybersecurity experts has risen substantially, while the mechanisms for raising the supply of such experts—education, recruitment, training, accession decisions—take time to reach fruition.

As a result, those who have such perceived cybersecurity skills benefit from a seller's market. Those who need people with cybersecurity skills pay higher prices or have unfilled positions. Within the U.S. federal government (e.g., within the Department of Defense [DoD]), the rising demand for cybersecurity skills cuts more sharply because government salaries are very difficult to change in the short term (it usually takes a promotion or a time-in-grade increase) and tend to be inflexible (in comparison to private salaries) even in the medium and long term. Thus, even as many proclaim the advent of cyberwar as a decisive component of modern warfare, others argue that DoD has a difficult time acquiring the people to wage that kind of war.

One underlying rationale for the rise in demand would be the growth in computers and connectivity. More data are stored and more processes are controlled in ways that are theoretically accessible, not least by the public, but also by insiders and via signals acquisition. Thus, the opportunity for mischief has grown, and with it, the size of the total risk. Still, Internet and digitization growth, at least in the United States, is robust but not as overtly vigorous as it was before the "dot-com" phenomenon peaked circa 2000. Taking that into account, another possible explanation is that finesse in developing tight, secure software has not advanced over the last five years, and thus the degree of insecurity has risen over and above the growth in the value of what is at risk. The evidence for that is mixed. Yes, the market has seen new vectors of attack (e.g., via cross-site scripting, mobile malware), but operating systems have more security features than they had five to ten years ago (most notably since the 2004 release or "necessary software security corrections" of Microsoft Windows XP Service Pack 2).[1] Another factor behind the suddenly rising demand for cybersecurity experts may be the advent of managed services, wherein a corporation outsources its information security and gauges return on investment against more costly security regimes that reduce user convenience.[2]

Another possible explanation is that, although the dependence *on* such systems and the vulnerability *of* such systems has not changed disproportionately over the last five years, the degree to which hackers *realize* the value of attacking networks has risen sharply. Thus, the threat has grown apace. But that explanation suggests its opposite: The problem is not so much that hackers have become more aware of the value that lies in networks but that defenders have become more aware of the hackers. The last few years have seen a steadily rising crescendo of *reports* on the consequences of being hacked,[3] notably the leakage of private information (e.g., one in South Carolina that exposed 3.5 million Social Security numbers—see Brown, 2012), and the large

---

[1]   Certain applications seem to be the source of fewer vulnerabilities over time, while others, notably Java and, to some extent, Adobe products, appear to have persistent weaknesses. See also Yang and Telang, 2008; and Ozment and Schechter, 2006.

[2]   These are two factors in a very complex process that may also include the number of vulnerabilities (per line of code), the ease with which those vulnerabilities could be exploited, and the existence of a larger attack surface (due to more devices and more different kinds of attacks).

[3]   This is a statement about perceptions, not the number or seriousness of hacks themselves. Reported data breaches appear to have declined in recent years. Systematic reporting began in 2005 and peaked several years later, followed by occasional increases. See Open Security Foundation, undated (note the dramatic increase in 2012 is most likely due to changes in data collection, specifically with regard to medical breaches). Other sources show similar results (e.g., Identity Theft Resource Center, 2013).

number of corporations that report having been penetrated by what is now labeled the advanced persistent threat (APT: often used to mean specific teams of Chinese hackers assigned to harvest intellectual property by establishing a persistent presence in the networks of U.S. and other technology targets). But cybercrimes are not the same as cybercrime reports. That the average interval between the start and the discovery of an APT is a year,[4] and that many, perhaps most, of these attacks are discovered by outside organizations (e.g., because they found the server that stolen corporate files are sitting on), suggests that many such attacks are *never* discovered. It is similarly possible that because of the heightened attention being paid to such attacks, the percentage of penetrations being discovered is going up—which, if true, would mean that the *apparent* volume of cyberattacks is rising. From a manpower perspective, all this introduces the possibility that the current demand for cybersecurity professionals has a strong perception component to it which may or may not accord to underlying realities. This hypothesis cannot, at least, be rejected out of hand. If true, it suggests that the demand for cybersecurity may fall in the longer term.

The Federal/Military Cybersecurity Workforce Problem

The relationship between the general problem of cybersecurity manpower and the particular challenge of national/homeland security access to the manpower is complex. Rising demand for a certain set of skills may manifest itself in different ways. In the private sector, rising demand is likely to be characterized by rising salaries, high rates of voluntary turnover (quits), and low rates of involuntary turnover (layoffs). In the public market, where wages and benefits are less flexible, rising demand is likely to be characterized, as well, by extended vacancies, a reduction in the quality of applicants (relative to requirements), and accelerated promotions (e.g., putting technical types into managerial

---

[4] "APT1 maintained access to victim networks for an average of 356 days. The longest time period APT1 maintained access to a victim's network was 1,764 days, or four years and ten months" (Mandiant, 2013).

slots prematurely). Normally, within acknowledged hierarchies such as the U.S. government, civilian and military managers are rewarded better than operators, and managers at comparable status levels are comparably paid—thereby putting downward pressure on the salary of scarce operators, however important their talents are. However, the federal government has learned how to make exceptions: doctors have their own pay bands, as do professors. Certain military occupational specialties carry bonuses. Of particular relevance to cybersecurity, certain categories of engineers at the National Security Agency have their own pay scale; this is an authority that the Department of Homeland Security has long sought.

DoD has given the nascent U.S. Cyber Command (through the U.S. Air Force, the executive agent and civilian personnel hiring authority) Section A authority to rapidly expand the civilian workforce. This allowed, for instance, the Air Force to make direct hires into federal service and offer recruits moving expenses and the repayment of student loans. For intelligence-related skill sets associated with cybersecurity, a military service can use the provisions of the Defense Civilian Personnel System (a special track in the civilian General Schedule) to offer similar recruitment incentives—if the functional manager of a skill set stipulates that incentives are necessary for competitive salary or living in a costly region of the country. Similarly, NSA and other agencies can apply a "Special Rate Table" of salaries at the GS-5 to GS-12 level (a boost of 44 percent to 24 percent above base salary, respectively) for computer scientists, information technology specialists, or engineers. Even though such measures make DoD a more attractive employer, the long recruitment, vetting, background checks, and security clearance can add months to the recruitment cycle and can discourage candidates.

Granted, federal employment comes with certain unique benefits. Employees serve the country, often considered a higher calling. Because the federal government is considered a long-term employer, it invests heavily in formal and informal training—an incentive for people to join the government when young so that they can then switch to private work when more experienced. Some parts of the government have a certain amount of cachet (e.g., the NSA). Finally, as a government employee, one can carry out certain operations that are illegal if done for anyone else. But there are also systematic downsides, notably in the military, with its belief in rotating warfighters among assignments in different locations in order to build sufficient breadth, particularly among officers. In a field that evolves as rapidly as cybersecurity, an absence of a few years while holding another job may be crippling, and the prospect of spending the most productive years outside the specialty may be discouraging.

Over the last 20 or more years, the government has finessed the problem of recruiting really skilled individuals by outsourcing the work they would have done to private contractors. The outsourcers can then pay market prices to deliver from qualified individuals services otherwise unavailable from direct employees.

But outsourcing does not solve all problems. First, many military and some civilian tasks cannot be performed by private contractors. Some of the reasons involve the hazards of being deployed in war zones or on warfare platforms (although these have loosened considerably over the last quarter century). More dominant are the legal issues associated with who can do what, many associated with the chain of military command. Second, it takes federal employees to oversee the contracting process—at very least to establish requirements, evaluate proposals, and select contractors. Oversight is important. It takes talent to write a good specification for contracted work, particularly if rapid changes in the environment suggest a corresponding requirement for rapid changes in what contractors are asked to do. If federal employees lack the skills to write such specifications (and particularly if the contractors understand as much), they are likely to be spending federal money inefficiently; hence, they cannot be supplanted. Third, outsourcing creates a vicious circle. If the "cool jobs" are given to contractors (Homeland Security Advisory Council, 2012), then extant and even prospective federal employees will have that much less motivation to stay or to join the federal government to work on cyber problems. This then reduces the quality of the federal labor pool, which then reinforces the initial tendency to assign the "cool jobs" to contractors.

Hence, a stable equilibrium in the national/international market for cybersecurity professionals can be consistent with unfilled positions in the federal market. This report therefore differentiates the global problem, so to speak, from the federal/military problem—while recognizing that these distinctions are hardly airtight.

Levels of the Game

The market for cybersecurity professionals is not a single market in which all items fetch the same price (as is, say, the market for diesel oil). There are broad definitions for cybersecurity and, consequently, many different cybersecurity jobs, whose requirements vary.[5] Of greater import is the vast difference between good and great hackers, almost to the point where they are different markets—and different people.

Some hackers (the best of the best)[6] are particularly good at finding vulnerabilities in software for purposes defensive (e.g., to make software less vulnerable and, importantly, the systems that use such software harder to attack) or offensive (e.g., to create tools that can be used to attack such systems). Others, also quite talented, are good at finding out whether and how a system has been attacked (notably by advanced persistent threats). At that high level of expertise, hackers may be born and not made (some of the most ingenious exploits have been developed by those "naturals" well under 18 years old—see Rosenblatt, 2011). That noted, the lone antisocial genius pursuing his or her wizardry is a well-worn trope that poorly describes how elite hacker *teams* function.[7] Nevertheless, to the extent that such skills are

---

[5] Many employment subcategories are driven by the increased attention to cybersecurity: for instance, certain types of lawyers are in high demand.

[6] By "hackers" we mean a savvy, curious, quick learner with natural ability to absorb technical information and techniques—and continuously improve the art of penetrating or protecting information systems.

[7] It has been broadly observed that the lone brilliant hacker is not necessarily the best acquisition for a security team. "Officials concede the need for a better, earlier, screening system to identify the right people to become cyberwarriors. There is at least one element on which both countries [Israel and the United States] agree. The intellectually arrogant, lone-ranger hacker is not the gold standard for innovative, multi-faceted cyberoperations" (Fulghum, 2012).

innate (or require a strong innate core to begin with) rather than simply taught, policies to increase training may be secondary to policies that discover promising individuals, encourage them to make cybersecurity a lifetime's work, provide them with educational opportunities, and inculcate them with requisite ethical norms.

The variegated labor market for cybersecurity (including for offensive cyberwar activities) suggests against solutions that ignore the great differences among skill levels, and how various inducements make a difference to different audiences (e.g., the heightened appeal of working for high-prestige groups in attracting the really skilled people—and retaining them with the gravitational pull of peer competition for innovative ideas). It also suggests caution when interpreting statements about the difficulties (or lack thereof) that organizations have in attracting cybersecurity professionals.

There are many problems that require the services of cybersecurity experts, but the one that causes the most difficult problems (e.g., cyber-espionage, cyber-sabotage) is malware, the ability of the attacker to issue arbitrary instructions to a system. A world without malware, were that possible, may well be a world in which there is less call for the efforts of the highest-status security experts and even all other cybersecurity professionals—notwithstanding the persistence of other security problems that arise from human error. This is not an absurd prospect. It is not a given that systems be built to host malware. Systems with all logic in hardware have no place to host persistent malware (that was not in the system when it left the factory). Systems that are not engineered to run user-supplied or -downloaded code on startup and practice now-common security techniques (address space layout randomization, for example) may also be relatively immune to malware. More broadly, an organization could weigh the relative cost of beefing up cybersecurity by hiring more talented individuals with adopting broad information system controls, such as isolating critical processes from the Internet, which may extract costs in one way (e.g., by increasing the difficulty of certain operations) while saving costs in another (e.g., by decreasing the urgency of hiring cybersecurity professionals).

CHAPTER TWO

What Others Have Observed

Although the current straits of the market for cybersecurity professionals did not arise the day the computer was invented, they were not newly discovered in 2014 either. Concerns that the nation would not be able to find enough people to protect its systems (and intrude upon those of its enemies) date back at least five years, to President Bush's Comprehensive National Cybersecurity Initiative (CNCI). Its eighth (unclassified) initiative out of 12 called to:

> *Expand cyber education.* While billions of dollars are being spent on new technologies to secure the U.S. Government in cyberspace, it is the people with the right knowledge, skills, and abilities to implement those technologies who will determine success. However there are not enough cybersecurity experts within the Federal Government or private sector to implement the CNCI, nor is there an adequately established Federal cybersecurity career field. Existing cybersecurity training and personnel development programs, while good, are limited in focus and lack unity of effort. In order to effectively ensure our continued technical advantage and future cybersecurity, we must develop a technologically-skilled and cyber-savvy workforce and an effective pipeline of future employees. It will take a national strategy, similar to the effort to upgrade science and mathematics education in the 1950's, to meet this challenge. (White House, undated)

Many of today's activities date back to the initiative, and the money allocated in support of that initiative. It is fair to observe that the solution to today's cybersecurity manpower problems would be considerably less far along had such efforts not been started then. Conversely, as with other large government-funded initiatives, one could posit that CNCI spawned a cyber educational-industrial complex that instinctively advocates for the need for the cybersecurity graduates moving through the pipeline. Nevertheless, the initiative has run its course, with funding now buried in the base budget of the agencies.

Similarly, reports of the difficulties of acquiring cybersecurity professionals have a history as well. In this chapter, we review the major reports—those carried out by the U.S. Government Accountability Office (GAO), BAH (formerly Booz-Allen Hamilton), DoD, and the Homeland Security Advisory Council—and then some of less major ones.

GAO, *Cybersecurity Human Capital: Initiatives Need Better Planning and Coordination*

GAO reports are a good place to start, because they tend to capture the conventional wisdom fairly well.[1]

This GAO report asserts on p. 5:

> Developing a strong workforce requires planning to acquire, develop, and retain it. Agency approaches to such planning can vary with the agency's particular needs and mission. Nevertheless, our own work and the work of other organizations, such as OPM [Office of Personnel Management], suggest that there are leading practices that workforce planning should address, such as:
>
> • Developing workforce plans that link to the agency's strategic plan. Among other things, these plans should identify activities required to carry out the goals and objectives of the agency's strategic plan and include analysis of the cur-

---

[1] GAO reports differ somewhat from others in that they tend to place great emphasis on process improvements, no one of which is controversial, rather than policy recommendations, which are more likely to require a higher level of analysis to justify.

rent workforce to meet long-term and short-term goals and objectives.
- Identifying the type and number of staff needed for an agency to achieve its mission and goals.
- Defining roles, responsibilities, skills, and competencies for key positions.
- Developing strategies to address recruiting needs and barriers to filling cybersecurity positions.
- Ensuring compensation incentives and flexibilities are effectively used to recruit and retain employees for key positions.
- Ensuring compensation systems are designed to help the agency compete for and retain the talent it needs to attain its goals.
- Establishing a training and development program that supports the competencies the agency needs to accomplish its mission.

Good workforce plans, GAO argues further, should involve top management, employees, and other stakeholders; determine critical skills and competencies; develop strategies that are tailored to address gaps in human capital approaches and critical skills and competencies; build the capability needed to address requirements to support workforce strategies; and monitor and evaluate the agency's progress.

The GAO report says that plans by themselves, however, will not be enough unless and until the time required to get professionals on board can be substantially reduced (p. 24):

DoD's Cyber Command reported that it can take a year to start a new employee because of both the lengthy hiring process and the time required to obtain a security clearance. . . . FBI reported continuing challenges with both obtaining initial clearances and processing clearances for cleared employees at other federal agencies that transfer to FBI. . . . We recently reported that agencies had made substantial progress in reducing the time to obtain security clearances and removed DOD's clearance process from our high-risk list in February 2011, but also reported that continuing work was needed in this area.

The report listed and reviewed the various initiatives that were begun to enhance the federal cybersecurity workforce (p. 34).

- The National Initiative for Cybersecurity Education (NICE) is an interagency effort coordinated by NIST [National Institute of Standards and Technology] to improve the nation's cybersecurity education, including efforts directed at the federal workforce. NIST has recently released a draft strategic plan for NICE for public comment, but the initiative lacks key details on activities to be accomplished and does not have clear authority to accomplish its goals. Nonetheless, the NICE definitions and roles for the cybersecurity workforce are well regarded within government, with US CYBER COMMAND and the Air Force A6/CIO voicing strong support.
- The CIO Council, NIST, OPM, and DHS all have separate efforts to develop a framework and models outlining cybersecurity roles, responsibilities, skills, and competencies. Officials reported plans to coordinate these efforts, but did not have specific time frames for doing so.
- The Information Systems Security Line of Business is a governmentwide initiative to create security training shared service centers. The effort is led by DHS and administered by DoD, the National Aeronautics and Space Administration (NASA), State, and VA [U.S. Department of Veterans Affairs]. Each center offers cybersecurity training for use by other agencies, but there are currently no plans to coordinate the centers' offerings or gather feedback on the training or incorporate lessons learned into revisions of the training.
- The IT Workforce Capability Assessment, administered by the CIO Council, is an effort to gather data on governmentwide IT training needs, including cybersecurity. The assessment is to occur every two years, but the CIO Council has no specific plans to use the results of the assessments.
- DHS and NSF's Scholarship for Service program provides funding for undergraduate and graduate cybersecurity education in exchange for a commitment by recipients to work for the federal government. Most agencies we reviewed stated they believed the program was valuable. However,

NSF currently does not track the longer-term value of the program by, for example, determining how many participants remain in government beyond their service commitment, but is working in an effort to develop and implement better ways to track this information.

Overall, it is GAO's contention that the current shortfalls in the acquisition and training of cybersecurity professionals require that more attention be paid to good management practice, a recommendation without cost implications as such. Although good management, almost by definition, never hurts, it is difficult to determine from GAO's reports whether even perfect management, given existing resources, can alleviate the problem substantially.

Partnership for Public Service and BAH, "Cyber IN-Security: Strengthening the Federal Cybersecurity Workforce"

This is one of the baseline documents in this field; it is widely cited (e.g., by the aforementioned GAO report). The writers argued that, "Our federal government will be unable to combat these threats without a more coordinated, sustained effort to increase cybersecurity expertise in the federal workforce. [Then-Secretary of Defense Robert] Gates has said the Pentagon is "desperately short of people who have capabilities (defensive and offensive cybersecurity war skills) in all the services and we have to address it."

The study was carried out, in large part, by using a survey instrument "conducted at 18 federal agencies and subcomponents that hire cybersecurity talent" (Partnership for Public Service and Booz Allen Hamilton, 2009, p. 2). Its key findings were:

- The governance of the current array of cybersecurity manpower programs is fragmented.
- Only a third of Chief Information Officers (CIOs) or Chief Information Security Officers (CISOs) were satisfied with the quantity/quality of job applicants. They were universally dissatisfied

with the U.S. Office of Personnel Management (OPM), but also not terribly pleased by the performance of their own human resource departments, too many of which were not particularly knowledgeable about the status of their hires' applications. A frustrated CIO at a major government department said his HR people "don't know the difference between good and bad candidates." . . . An agency HR official said, in defense, that hiring managers and CIOs "don't always understand that it must be a fair and open application process."

- Hiring rules were complex. More than three-quarters of the CIO/CISOs (or other information technology hiring managers) were dissatisfied or very dissatisfied with the time required to close the deal and hire someone. By contrast, getting a contractor on the job was quite easy (one DHS office was observed to be mostly contractors).
- The Scholarships-for-Service (SFS) program, which generated 120 graduates a year (the Information Assurance Scholarship Program [IASP] program graduated an additional 30 individuals), could easily generate a thousand such graduates. However, scholarships for service are intended to generate skilled graduates who will enter the federal or government-sponsored workforce. In the face of sequestration, most graduates were released from this commitment due to a pause in government hiring and were allowed to find work with government contractors.
- The ability to hire varied by agency. One human resources professional observed, "We are outbid by other agencies—FBI, NSA, DHS. They have gotten exceptions where they can hire at any level . . . people jump ship and go to NSA."
- There were several recommendations (more precisely, recommendation groups), addressed to the White House, the Office of Personnel Management, and Congress, respectively.
- The White House was called on to develop a cybersecurity manpower blueprint, devise an updated set of job classifications, and mount the bully pulpit to enlist the support of the private sector and academia to enhance America's STEM (science, technology, engineering, and mathematics) talent pool.

- OPM, for its part, was called on to create a high-level team to remove barriers related to recruiting, hiring, and retention—or, more generally, to "fix" the federal hiring process or at least give the various agencies greater flexibility to fix their own. It needed to establish an "idea clearinghouse"; collect, analyze, and use agency-specific data on new hires; and expand the number of universities offering curricula in cybersecurity and information assurance (not clear how). OPM was also tasked with resolving longstanding problems about classification and position descriptions; expediting the security-clearance process; and working with the intelligence community and non-intelligence agencies to define a career path for cybersecurity specialists.
- The various agencies were told they should implement the Total Talent Management Model with its five phases: (1) sourcing and recruitment, (2) job announcements, (3) selecting the right talent and closing the deal, (4) getting these people on board expeditiously, and (5) retaining them.
- Congress, in turn, should force OPM to report on its progress in meeting goals and put more money into training and development, not least by putting more money into scholarships.

This report, similar to the GAO report, emphasized management but not an increase in resources, except (by implication) for the SFS program. These authors would increase the emphasis on assiduously working the cybersecurity professional problem rather than improving management up to some abstract standard of excellence (as GAO favors)—but the difference between the two is a subtle one.

CSIS Commission on Cybersecurity for the 44th Presidency, "A Human Capital Crisis in Cybersecurity"

This is another well-cited report (by the GAO et al.) on cybersecurity manpower, more willing to make a strong argument than the previous two.

Several themes play throughout the report. One is the difference that having really good cybersecurity professionals makes to an organization's ability to keep its systems free from problems. It compared, for instance, the Departments of Commerce and State, both of whose systems were compliant with standards arising from the Federal Information Security Management Act but used software (inevitably) vulnerable to zero-day attacks: "By contrast, the DOS [Department of State] witness [indicated that the Department] . . . had built a team of network forensics investigators, deep-packet-analysis experts and security programmers who could find and eliminate problems," [so that they] "found the attack within moments after it had occurred." By way of reinforcement it cited the testimony of the Defense Information Systems Agency (DISA)'s Richard Hale to the effect that units that are overly dependent on security tools rarely find the APT, while those that have deep and broad technical security skills and constantly adapt the tools to changing threat patterns are the ones that immediately identify and eliminate the APT.

The problem, the report argued, was one of quality. One of its more vivid observations was from Jim Gosler, who opined that there were about a thousand security people in the United States who have the specialized security skills to operate effectively in cyberspace. By contrast, Gosler added, we need 10,000 to 30,000 of them. Two years earlier, Lt. Gen Croom (then JTF-GNO) had observed, "I cannot get the technical security people I need." The report concluded, "We not only have a shortage of the highly technically skilled people required to operate and support systems we have already deployed, we also face an even more desperate shortage of people who can design security systems, write safe computer code, and create the ever-more sophisticated tools needed to prevent, detect, mitigate, and reconstitute systems after an attack."

The report found that the match between the formal credentials of cybersecurity workers and what they really needed was poor. Current credentials, the report observed, were weakly coordinated with competence. Furthermore, although Association for Computing Machinery (ACM) opposed licensing software engineers, there was, according to the report, little controversy about the need for greater professionalization (demonstrated competence in a defined body of knowledge plus ethics). Any programmer, for instance, who does not follow basic rules, such as avoiding the 25 most serious coding mistakes (as defined by MITRE), would be a threat to his employers and to those who use computers connected to systems running such software. This led to a strong endorsement of a unified (rather than federated) certification system as being not only necessary but sustainable.

Yet, as the report observed, progress was under way. The federal government was already moving in the right direction. Professional bodies such as ISACA (Information Systems Audit and Control Association), the SANS Institute (a training organization), CREST (Council of Registered Ethical Security Testers), and IEEE (Institute for Electrical and Electronic Engineering) were making important contributions. DHS was already building an "Essential Body of Knowledge" and working on defining CISSP (certified information system security professional) standards. The FBI was training cybersecurity law enforcement officers. NSA had established Centers of Academic Excellence. DoD's Information Assurance Workforce Improvement Program was under way and developing its 2010 updates.[2] There were also a series of contests, including US Cyber Challenge, the Cyber Security Treasure Hunt, CyberPatriot, NetWars, and the DC3 (Defense Cyber Crime Center) Digital Forensics Challenge.

In general, the authors argued that there were four elements of any strategy to deal with the challenge:

- Promote and fund more rigorous curricula (as NSF and NSA are pursuing).
- Support technically rigorous professional certifications that include a tough educational component and a monitored practical component.

---

[2] U.S. Department of Defense Manual, 2012. This directive mandates that would-be experts on information assurance receive specific certifications. As of this writing the National Research Council is examining whether mandates are a good idea.

- Use a combination of the hiring process, the acquisition process, and training resources to raise the level of technical competence of those who build, operate, and defend governmental systems.
- Assure there is a career path for such professionals at both the civilian (e.g., civil service) and military level.

The Center for Strategic and International Studies (CSIS) Commission report's specific recommendations were as follows:

- ·DHS needed to generate a taxonomy of cyber roles and skills. The Bureau of Labor Statistics, similarly, needed to develop Standard Occupational Classifications for the cybersecurity workforce.
- The Office of Management and Budget (OMB) and NIST, working together, should explore licensing requirements.
- In acquiring information technology, agencies should include the appropriate IT security configurations available from checklists.nist.gov.
- OPM should manage careers path structures better.
- DHS should create a Cyber Corps Alumni Group.

The CSIS report, like the previous two, did not argue for spending much more money so much as it argued for more efficient management, with particular attention to developing a more rigorous process for qualifying cybersecurity professionals and ensuring that qualified professionals had a secure and upward-moving career path within or at least working with the federal government. The potential disjunction between the seriousness with which these reports regard the problem and the paucity of recommendations with serious resource implications seems anomalous and only partially explained by the austere spirit of the times.

DoD, *Cyber Operations Personnel Report*

This is the closest to an official report on the cybersecurity manpower available to defend national security. One fact that stands out clearly is the difficulty in actually counting cybersecurity employees. DoD's direct count as of 2009 was roughly 4,000 for defensive operations and 14,000 for information assurance. By contrast, the count provided for FISMA compliance was a much higher 46,000. The latter, however, counts contractors: DoD civilians and contractors in 2009 constituted just over half of the reported workforce in the latter.

Another fact is how much the ability to satisfy cybersecurity manpower needs varies by service and component. The Army reported insufficient personnel within U.S. Army Intelligence and Security Command (INSCOM) and was working on a plan to grow capacity in fiscal year 2012 and beyond. In addition, they cited concerns that personnel strength was insufficient when Informations Operations Condition (INFOCON) was raised. The Marine Corps noted gaps in cyber planners, source analysts focusing on the cyberspace domain, and mid-level certified IA technical managers. The Joint Staff and five of the Combatant Commands identified insufficient numbers of personnel, with U.S. Special Operations Command (SOCOM) citing a significant increase in requirements and U.S. European Command (EUCOM) stating that shortfalls impacted their ability to train, share, and engage NATO and foreign partners in cyber defense.

One confounding factor in attracting cybersecurity professionals is that DoD, at least as of that point, had yet to fully exploit its ability to compensate these hard-to-find workers for their talents. Among schedule-2210 civilians, for instance, only 2 percent were GS-15s and 12 percent were GS-14s. Among enlisted ranks, E-8s and E-9s are similarly scarce. Enlistment bonuses were not vigorously used either. The higher bonuses in fiscal year 2009 typically went to individuals in the nuclear field, advanced electronics, linguists, special warfare, and special operations fields such as explosive ordnance disposal (EOD). There were some cyber-related bonuses from the Army and Marines but not USAF (the U.S. Navy is not mentioned either way). There are also reenlisted bonuses, and Critical Skills Retention Bonus(es), but the amount of money put against these bonuses was similarly limited.

DoD was more actively using resources to promote intake (as opposed to retention). Internships included "Federal Career Intern Program," "Student Career Experience Program," and "Student

Temporary Experience Program." However, a recent ruling by the Merit Systems Protection Board in November 2010 had found that Federal Career Intern Program (FCIP) violated veterans' preferences rules, and the authority had been eliminated as of March 2011. Before the program ended, it had reduced hiring time by as much as 60 percent.

There were also several initiatives under way as of that writing:

- DoD sought expedited hiring authority, notably for the five occupational series that accounted for the bulk of the manpower: IT management, computer science, computer engineering, electric engineering, and telecommunication specialist.
- IASP funding was increased.
- A centrally managed cyber workforce loan repayment program was developed.
- The value of IT Special Salary Rates was restored.
- Certification bonuses for information technology and cybersecurity certification were created.
- Education was beefed up through the establishment of the iCollege, the addition of other schoolhouses, and improvements in training in such schoolhouses.

Homeland Security Advisory Council, *CyberSkills Task Force Report*

This report merits particular mention not only because of its unique recommendations but because of its distinguished committee members. They included Jeff Moss, the founder of DEF CON (an annual hacker conference), and Alan Paller, who runs SANS. The council focused on why DHS was having difficulties finding the cybersecurity manpower it needed. It concluded that DHS was caught in a vicious cycle: Because of its difficulties in finding the better cybersecurity professionals, those who were hired did not get the interesting and challenging work assignments—the "cool jobs." As a result, DHS was not viewed as a "cool" place to work, which made it uncompetitive for finding such professionals. Thus, running as a thread through these recommendations is the importance of DHS reserving the "cool jobs" for civil servants as a way of attracting good people to work for DHS and retaining them once they are there. By way of confirmation, Roberta Stempfley, a senior cybersecurity official at DHS, noted that she had a handful of highly talented "ninjas" on her staff, driven by positive peer competition, striving to be on top of their game. She said she could use more than a handful—perhaps a dozen—with the intent that any new hires to her highly talented team would be vetted/hired by her ninjas already on board.

The council concluded with a long list of recommendations for DHS:

- Keep an authoritative list of mission-critical cybersecurity tasks.
- Develop training scenarios and a model to evaluate on-board talent against these tasks.
- Establish a "Cyberworkforce Board" to manage workforce development.
- Make cybersecurity jobs attractive.
- Establish community-college programs to identify and train cybersecurity workers.
- Raise the eligibility criteria for Centers of Academic Excellence and Scholarship for Service schools.
- Encourage veterans to apply for cybersecurity jobs.
- Use excepted service authority vigorously for hiring.
- Specify mission-critical skills within DHS solicitations (e.g., requests for proposals).
- Establish a pilot DHS CyberReserve program.

The subtleties of the argument in favor of reserving "cool jobs" for civil servants so that working at DHS can be considered "cool" raises the question of what the nation loses if "cool" people do the "cool jobs" for contractors rather than for DHS itself.

Amyas Morse, *The UK Cyber Security Strategy: Landscape Review*

This report is a reminder that difficulties in finding enough good cybersecurity professionals are, unsurprisingly, global. Information architectures (e.g., their dependence on Microsoft's operating systems) are the same around the world; the opportunities for mischief in cyberspace know no boundaries; many of the private enterprises affected by what happens in cyberspace are themselves global; and the market for cybersecurity professionals is becoming increasingly global, not only because such professionals are mobile and scarce enough to be in demand everywhere, but because many of them can have global effects without leaving home at all. The United Kingdom's cyber problems are not so different from those of the United States.

The report emphasized ensuring the United Kingdom has enough skilled people and the right research and development to plug the immediate skills gap and address longer-term needs in the public and private sector. According to its authors, "the number of ICT and cyber security professionals in the UK has not increased in line with the growth of the internet. This shortage of ICT skills hampers the UK's ability to protect itself in cyberspace and promote the use of the internet both now and in the future." This skills, the report added, are not only technical but include those of "softer" scientists such as "psychologists; law enforcers; corporate strategists and risk managers."

The United Kingdom's Minister for Business, Innovation and Skills was quoted referring to a "decade-long" decline in computer science education (in other words, since the "dot-com" boom ended), and the United Kingdom's special representative to business for cybersecurity also commented on the lack of younger people working in the area of cybersecurity. The report continued, "Interviews with government, academia and business representatives confirmed that the UK lacks technical skills and that the current pipeline of graduates and practitioners would not meet demand. Those we interviewed from academia considered that it could take up to 20 years to address the skills gap at all levels of education."

Other Articles

David M. Hollis argued in *Small Wars Journal* that the "capabilities of the military's Reserve Components are not effectively utilized to conduct and support cyberspace domain operations" (Hollis, 2011), particularly in contrast to China's use of specialists as reservists (e.g., chemical professionals within chemical warfare units) notably for cyberspace operations. He proposed cadres that would (1) inspect the critical infrastructure, (2) assist in mediation and repair, (3) conduct missions to increase infrastructure resilience, (4) respond to major incidents by leveraging TS-SCI insights into the threat, (5) advise state, local, tribal, and territorial governments, and (6) stand by for mobilization into main warfighting force.

A National Defense University (NDU) report observed that in updating its directive on information security, DoD came to require that its computer network defenders pass Certified Ethical Hacker certification from the International Council of E-commerce Consultants (Starr, Kuehl, and Pudas, 2010). The authors concluded in favor of creating and/or expanding competitions to find promising candidates, as well as carrying out "whole-of-government" exercises.

In *Human Capital Management for the USAF Cyber Force*, Lynn Scott et al. (2010) asked what kind of capabilities the Air Force needed, where they should be, who needed what skills, and how changing the Air Force Specialty Code (AFSC) might help get the right people to the right place. The report recommended (1) a more comprehensive concept of operations (CONOPS) for cyberspace operations, (2) converting such a CONOPS into a total force human capital requirement, (3) establishing a lateral-officer AFSC, (4) retooling the enlisted communications-computer specialty into an accession-entry cyber specialty, and (5) continually reassessing the cyber force's sustainability.

"Enhancing the Cybersecurity Workforce," by Michael Assante and David Tobey (2011), asserted that (1) a capable cybersecurity professional would need to put in at least 10,000 hours practicing the trade, (2) skills could not be confused with knowledge, and (3) having defenders think like attackers was a critical skill.

Conclusions

A consistent theme that runs through these reports is the notion of a crisis in the market for cybersecurity professionals (albeit without much assessment of exactly what the inability to hire enough such professionals means for cybersecurity itself). This is coupled with a recitation of the various government programs meant to alleviate such perceived shortages, and, in many cases, a suggested list of approaches to enhance or at least increase the level of government assistance in attracting potential employees to this profession and educating them when they get there. Several reports suggested changing management practices to allow potential employers to focus on the requirements for finding and keeping enough of the right kind of cybersecurity professionals (the latter to be determined by rigorous standards). However, it is by no means clear that improvement in management practices would have any more than second-order benefits in the face of what are, for potential employers, difficult labor market fundamentals.

CHAPTER THREE

Findings from Interviews and Statistics

To build up an empirical record in furtherance of prior studies and in support of theoretical considerations, we carried out semi-structured interviews with representatives of five U.S. government organizations, five education institutions, two security companies, one defense firm, and one outside expert.[1] What follows is based on these interviews, supplemented as necessary by other material and coupled with analysis as needed to address particular issues.

This section is organized into three topic areas: the experience of large employers of cybersecurity professionals, the perspective from the schoolhouse, and a treatment of particular issues and related policy options.

---

[1] We used two sets of interview questions: one for those looking for cybersecurity professionals; the other for those who educate them. These questions were used not as parts of survey instruments but as departure points for conversation. For employers we asked about: the demographics of their current workforce; the skill sets that were most often called for and those that were hardest to acquire; how they assessed the call for such skills; the time horizons they employed; how they chose between internal training and external recruitment; how their training programs worked; and what public policies they would advocate to help them meet their cybersecurity needs. For educators we asked: what their curriculum emphasized; the general and cyber-related skill sets of their incoming students; their distribution into military, civilian and foreign; the jobs their student took after graduating; partnerships between the school and potential employers; the skills they thought future employers valued most; and what public policies they would advocate to help them meet their cybersecurity needs.

How Employers Meet their Need for Cybersecurity Professionals

Organizations, particularly large ones, have various ways of finding cybersecurity professionals. How they deal with the challenges varies widely, based in large part on what assets each organization can bring to bear. But, overall, they do appear to cope, one way or the other.

One large defense contractor (roughly 100,000 employees) indicated that it concentrates on internal recruitment to fill its cybersecurity needs. Large defense contractors have an advantage in that their work forces are quite technically adept. This particular company notes that half its employees are already scientists or engineers, which provides a solid base to start with. From that base the contractor creates its own training regimen and puts thousands of employees through a two-week course. The talented ones, as defined by their performance and behavior (rather than their prior education—a standout could be an English major with passion and curiosity) are sent through further education, culminating in six to nine months of focused training. Currently, about two thousand employees are considered to be cybersecurity professionals. One reason the company emphasizes internal training so heavily is that there is, in fact, a dearth of good people from the outside from whom to select. By contrast, since every employee has to have some cybersecurity training to bring the company's cybersecurity up to some standard, the company reaps the secondary benefit of using such training to identify potential cybersecurity workers.

One of its thrusts is developing a predictive capability for cyberattacks. It focuses on determining exactly who is interested in going after its trade secrets, what their *modus operandi* is, in what order they select targets, and what techniques they use to penetrate organizations and exfiltrate their data. This capability allows the company to analyze each (discovered) intrusion and analyze its malware and its command-and-control. At this point investigators now have ten years' worth of data to work with. Another thrust is to model the attacker's "kill chain" as a series of six basic steps: reconnaissance, identifying a vulnerability, identifying a weapon, weapons delivery, performance monitoring, and command-and-control (Hutchins, Clopperty, and Amin,

2010). This allows them to develop an approach that works against each or all of the six as a way of reducing to negligible levels the odds that an attacker will succeed. This, in turn, creates a counter-attacking task list, which then informs the corporation what skills are needed to execute the task list, which in turn, guides the conversion of technical employees into cybersecurity employees. As with NSA (see below), this company argues that it has found ways to keep its best cybersecurity people on board by giving them interesting missions, reinforced by the notion that big companies can do big things.

NSA

The NSA is the country's largest and leading employer of cybersecurity professionals. In the face of the current stresses in the market for such professionals, officials there believe they are doing quite well—fewer than 1 percent of their positions are vacant for any significant length of time, and supervisors, queried after their new hires have been working for six months, report being very happy with the personnel they get. NSA also has a very low turnover rate (losing no more to voluntary quits than to retirements). One reason is that it pays attention to senior technical development programs to ensure that employees stay current and engaged.

Yet, to get to that point, our interview indicates that NSA must and does pay a great deal of attention to workforce issues. If not its primary focus, then it is still very high up on the list. Although only 80 people have recruitment as their full-time occupation, another 300 have recruitment as an additional duty, and another 1,500 beyond that are involved in the whole recruitment and employment process. All told, that is a great deal of effort—suggesting, from our perspective, that the difficulties of finding enough cybersecurity professionals can be largely met if sufficient energy is devoted to the task. NSA has outreach into many universities, not simply those designated its Centers of Academic Excellence (CAE),[2] although it pays attention to support-

---

[2] In 2012, NSA designated four universities (out of over 20 applicants) as Centers of Academic Excellence in Cyber Operations: the Naval Postgraduate School, Dakota State University, Northeastern University, and University of Tulsa.

ing cybersecurity curricula development in the CAE schools, as noted. In some cases it has people teaching in schools to encourage potential cybersecurity professionals at the pre-college levels, particularly, for obvious reasons, in the state of Maryland.

For the most part, our interview suggests that the NSA makes rather than buys cybersecurity professionals, although its recruitment process is very sensitive to the importance of determining those qualities that predispose people to make good employees. Recruiters also look hard at schools that have a reputation for educating people that go into the military. Fully 80 percent of their hires are entry level, the vast majority of whom have bachelor's degrees. They could conceivably draw deeper by finding particularly talented junior college graduates, but the latter would have to undergo a much longer training program as a result. Furthermore, they are not inclined to look for the brilliant nondegreed hacker.[3]

NSA has a very intensive internal schooling system, lasting as long as three years for some. This too, would be difficult for other institutions to duplicate. NSA can take advantage not only of its size, but also of its low turnover rate. The latter means that it reaps the benefits of its investments in people rather than seeing the benefits accrue to other organizations after NSA has paid the costs of the training (not least of which is the time that such students spend off the job to be trained). Employers with more turnover may logically deem it not worthwhile investing that much to educate their employees.

In all fairness, only one organization can be the most prestigious place to work, and for this line of work (and for this size of organization), NSA is hard to beat. It consistently absorbs a third of all Scholarship for Service graduates, as shown in Figure 3.1,[4] in part because

---

[3] There is advocacy for the idea that the federal government should seek out raw genius among the population, even in the absence of formal education or presence of divergent lifestyles, and not worry too much about whether recruits can pass standard criteria for getting security clearances. The recent (June 2013) example of Edward Snowden, who divulged many of NSA's secrets and pulled down salaries of well over $100,000 a year without even a high school diploma (or General Educational Development equivalent), is unlikely to bolster that argument.

[4] Homeland Security Advisory Council (2012, p. 12); information from an email from Victor Piotrowski, SFS program manager at NSF, current as of March 15, 2012. The SFS

Figure 3.1
Where SFS Graduates Go to Work

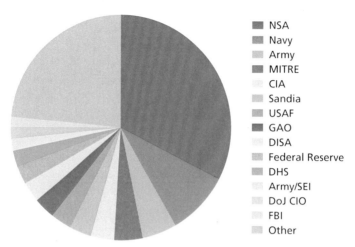

- NSA
- Navy
- Army
- MITRE
- CIA
- Sandia
- USAF
- GAO
- DISA
- Federal Reserve
- DHS
- Army/SEI
- DoJ CIO
- FBI
- Other

SOURCE: Homeland Security Advisory Council, 2012.
RAND *RR430-3.1*

it has the most job openings but also because it has a reputation for hiring the best hackers.

Central Intelligence Agency

CIA, a mission-partner of NSA, indicated that it also builds talent from within. For its intake, the Agency uses academic credentials (the preferred minimum is a Master's degree in a cyber field) amplified by a personal interview protocol. The candidate's innate driving interest to understand what goes on within computer applications—the passion to understand how the software works inside the computer game, not just play the game—is a key attribute of the interview because it helps to describe "gratification" for the candidate.

Candidates are sought in job fairs (the table banner might ask "at what age did you take apart the family computer?") as well as hacker conventions (e.g., Black Hat or DEF CON). They are also drawn from the inbound new hires for the CIA's IT Department, approached and

program is the largest government-funded scholarship program.

interviewed on the prospect of moving from supporting networks to exploiting and defending cyber missions. Here, it is worth noting that both the Navy and NSA have outsourced their IT infrastructure in search of near-term savings, but at the cost of losing the talent pool, particularly at the junior level, from which they can draw cyber warriors. By contrast, other military services and national agencies have the opportunity to find the sharp diamonds within their ranks.

According to our interviews, the agency believes it is aggressively looking for cybersecurity professionals both internally and externally. Yet, obstinate challenges persist in identifying, vetting, and hiring new employees in several high-end cyber workforce skill areas, namely cloud engineering and the esoteric fields of multilevel cross-domain security and network resiliency engineering.

USCYBERCOM

USCYBERCOM is using the precepts of the Defense Language Aptitude Test (DLAT), which infers a military recruit's natural ability to work with foreign languages. Analogously, USCYBERCOM is fielding a testing regimen that identifies those who can hurdle a high bar to enter a candidacy to an eventual varsity game of cybersecurity maneuver. Using feeder streams of recruits who move through service component education and on-the-job-training, USCYBERCOM plans to build teams of Cyber Protection Platoons that will be certified through mission-assurance training. A significant challenge, they believe, will be developing appropriate job qualifications and currency standards for a cyber warrior, determining how to certify those skills in intense combat, field exercises, and the practical inclusion of reserve component skills. Certification requirements are included in the Command's Cyber Skills Development Plan and accompanying course catalog. Military and civilian members of the Command and associated service components will be issued Individual Development Plans.

Concomitantly, DoD is implementing a new architecture (the Joint Information Environment), a cloud-based consolidation of the .mil network. This architecture requires a new and parallel regimen of cybersecurity training. The move to cloud-based services—believed to be a more secure environment—could recast the skills required by cybersecurity warriors, from scanning and patching networks to the management of mobile devices and data access controls. The DoD Joint Information Environment (JIE) comprises a shared infrastructure, enterprise services, and a single security architecture to improve mission effectiveness, increase security, and realize information technology (IT) efficiencies. The JIE will be the base from which DoD can operate in the knowledge that data are safe from adversaries (Alexander, 2013). This initiative was designed to fundamentally change the DoD Information Network (DoDIN). It consolidates and standardizes functions and data centers to help move DoD to a cloud-based architecture. Such consolidation will require a new and parallel regimen of cybersecurity training and alter DoD's requirements for cybersecurity skills, in large part, by homogenizing training and skill-set requirements across the various services, thereby removing the limits on portability of service members.

JIE should permit DoD to *eventually* get by with fewer cybersecurity workers.[5] In the interim, though, there may be a bulge in the workforce pipeline, with a requirement for a sustaining workforce to secure legacy service networks and while training the new workforce for the JIE.

USAF

The U.S. Air Force is another large organization with a substantial need for cybersecurity expertise and an expectation that turnover will be low among its employees and, hence, that internal education is a cost-effective way of meeting its needs. Accordingly, the USAF has taken a very systematic approach that involves, first, an attempt to delineate the tasks it needs, and second, an attempt to convert the tasks into workload and skills requirement. This calculation, in turn, informs how many people it wishes to pull into their schoolhouse system (which, in turn, generates internal estimates for how many schoolhouses its needs).

Our interviews indicate that the USAF has a systematic way of determining who would best fill its cybersecurity missions, which it

---

[5] By way of analogy, see Davidson (2013).

divides into A-Shred, which can include some upper-tier profession-als, and B-Shred, whose duties are more strictly defined. To get into either Shred requires passing some basic ICT (information-communi-cations technology) "literacy" tests. For many officers, a communica-tions degree is a must. However, the process of getting into the A-Shred category entails more hand-picking, with degrees playing a smaller role in determining who is considered part of which Shred. Among the enlisted cadres, the Air Force is in sufficiently good shape that there is now a waiting list to be considered for a cybersecurity AFSC.

Conversations with Air Force managers suggest that they are fairly satisfied that they can get their basic cybersecurity needs met, but this may be true, in our observation, because they do not rely on attracting upper-tier professionals to do so. Whether this is because they truly do not need such individuals or because they do not realize they do need such individuals is something we could not determine. Furthermore, there is also a contradiction between the Air Force's confidence in its military accession programs and the fact that it is using more civil-ians (and correspondingly fewer military personnel) for cybersecurity than its goals suggest. The USCYBERCOM guidance to its service components was to strive for a force mix of 80 percent military and 20 percent civilian, but the Air Force and other components find them-selves running 60 percent military, 30 percent civilian, and 10 percent contractors. Perhaps the Air Force is constantly overoptimistic about its ability to fill positions with scarce military personnel—or perhaps the Air Force has found that it is very difficult in too many cases to find someone with adequate capabilities to fill positions, and civilians have to be sought instead.

The Role of Education

Difficulties in finding good cybersecurity professionals, the increased recognition of the cybersecurity problem (particularly since 2007), and rising salary levels for cybersecurity professionals have prompted the creation of cybersecurity concentrations in various schools across the nation.

Cybersecurity Programs

The six educational institutions we looked at varied widely. One has made a specialty of examining the link between cybersecurity and chemical processes (the motivating incident being the Bhopal chemical leak and how to ensure against something like that happening again). Another offers a more traditionally academic curriculum but with a strong interest in the challenges of cybersecurity as networks scale toward and beyond a million nodes. A third is housed at an academic institution but largely caters to the continuing education market, notably for managers who need to translate findings generated by technical professionals to a form that can be understood by higher layers of management. A fourth operates a more traditional computer-science curriculum but last year started a cybersecurity major. Its core competence arises from its closeness to the Washington decisionmaking apparatus. The fifth institution, the U.S. Naval Academy, is starting a cybersecurity major next year (the class of 2016); its specialty is serving Navy needs. Finally, we talked to SANS, an organization that offers non-degree educational courses targeted at those who have already had exposure to cybersecurity and want to bring their game to the next level.

The composition of the student body similarly varies. At one school, all the students must be able to get a security clearance (at a minimum, therefore, they must be citizens). At the U.S. Naval Academy (USNA), all upper class students already have security clearances. In the third program, the emphasis on continuing education means that most of the students already have security clearances. The two other schools (and SANS) have no such requirement. In the traditional degree-granting program, a high percentage of the students are foreign, but many stay in the United States, and some of those who return to their home country end up working for the overseas offices of U.S. multinationals. At SANS, 88 percent of alumni are North American. Active service members are very well represented in these schoolhouses.

The USNA's program is illustrative. Its first cohort of cyber operations majors consists of three dozen midshipmen, roughly 3 percent of the total class. The extent to which this new major will actually increase the supply of cybersecurity professionals (in the capacity of hackers) should be understood in its context: Graduates of service academies are military officers first, and subject-matter professionals second. Accordingly, most of the courses these cybersecurity majors take will be in the core curriculum that all midshipmen take; many of the major-related courses are expected to resemble their counterparts within the computer science department, albeit with a greater emphasis on the security aspects of information technology. In addition, there will be course offerings associated with the management of computer security: e.g., policy, law, and psychology. As such, this major is more likely to produce intelligent and sophisticated employers of cybersecurity professionals rather than the hackers themselves. Incidentally, this major follows recently instituted requirements that *all* midshipmen take two classes in cybersecurity.

According to our interviews, none of the educational institutions had difficulty in attracting instructors who might otherwise be attracted to doing cybersecurity and garnering high salaries rather than teaching it and earning professors' salaries. This may arise from the fact that instructors tend to be more mature and are not necessarily hacker hotshots. Another factor is that many schools can meet many of their educational requirements by using adjuncts (particularly in the Washington, D.C., area).

The NSA does get heavily involved in cybersecurity curricula in general, but rarely in particular. The general thrust is to work with its several Centers of Academic Excellence to generate a consolidated curriculum, but work on such a curriculum is potentially controversial (as schools specialize) and nowhere near complete.

Finally, at least one respondent mentioned the profusion of those offering education and training services, starting with little more than a brochure. This would seem to be a case of demand (for educational services) creating supply, but not necessarily at sufficiently high levels of competence.

Our sense is that the current expansion of educational opportunities is exactly what one would expect to see given the expanding opportunities and rising wages in the cybersecurity market—coupled with the high degree of active government involvement in terms of scholarships, summer internships, close interworking relationships, and, more rarely, direct grants. One respondent suggested that the greater provision of equipment (e.g., latest-generation routers) whose security parameters they could learn and tweak would be useful.

Overall Statistics

Enrollment figures in North American computer departments are consistent with changes in labor market conditions. According to the Taulbee Survey,[6] the average number of enrollees per computer science department dropped from 400 at the height of the dot-com boom to 200 in 2007 but then rebounded strongly to 300 in 2012 (the latest year surveyed). The number of computer science departments in the United States rose from 176 to 189 between 2007 and 2012. The number of graduates, which, not surprisingly, lags the number of enrolled students by two years, peaked at around 20,000 between 2001 and 2003 and then fell to below 10,000 in 2009 before rebounding sharply to just fewer than 15,000 projected in 2013. The total number of computer science graduates (all three levels) doubled from 1998 to 2004, then fell to 1.4 times 1998 levels circa 2007 and by 2011 had recovered to 1.6 times 1998 levels.

Ph.D. production, a variable that lags even further behind events (and responds to developments in academia as well as industry) stayed constant between 1995 and 2003 (roughly 900 a year), doubled by 2008 and held that level before touching its all-time peak in 2012. The conclusion from these data is what theory would predict: Educational enrollment reflects market conditions, but with a lag measured in years. Granted, 60 percent of all Ph.D. students are nonresident aliens, but of all Ph.D.'s produced, only 10 percent of them found their next jobs overseas. The current burgeoning market for cybersecurity

---

6   The annual Taulbee Survey, conducted by the Computing Research Association (CRA), surveys academic computer science/engineering departments in North America to discern trends in the student body and faculty. Although participation is less than complete (as it is in NSF surveys), annual participation rates are roughly in the 70 percent range. See Zweben and Bizot, 2013. Actual participation rates vary (and no attempt is made to estimate statistics from non-respondents); they were closer to 80 percent from 2000 to 2007. For this reason, gross Taulbee numbers (in comparison to per department numbers) after 2007 may understate the number of computer science majors.

professionals may prove to be as large a driver as the dot-com boom was, although the statistics to indicate as much are off into the future.

Many of these educational trends can be explained by labor force trends. Although the demand for cybersecurity professionals has never been greater, the overall demand for those with a computer science education (from which cybersecurity professionals were drawn prior to specialized training) has yet to return to the levels associated with the dot-com boom. Information technology employment has just barely returned to its levels during the boom, and as of 2011, computer programmer salaries were still below levels reached in 2000 (Salzman, Kuehn, and Lowell, 2013). In the following chapter, we discuss labor market forces through the lens of the labor economics and personnel economics literature.

CHAPTER FOUR

The Economics of the Cybersecurity Labor Market

In this chapter, we review some of the insights from the fields of labor economics and personnel economics, to shed light on facts we observe in the labor market for cybersecurity professionals.[1] We begin with a simplified view of how fundamental market forces may explain recent empirical observations about the cybersecurity workforce. We then turn to a number of important factors that complicate this simplified view, including differences in human capital and constraints on the federal government's ability to raise wages.

A Simplified View of the Labor Market for Cyberprofessionals

Figure 4.1 presents a simplified view of the labor market for cybersecurity professionals. In the recent past—2007 is probably a good base year to consider—the supply of cybersecurity professionals, and

---

[1] There is substantial overlap between labor and personnel economics, but they can broadly be distinguished as follows. Labor economics uses systematic theory to explain important empirical facts about the labor market. The literature covers the classic topics of labor demand, labor supply, and their effect on the wage structure. It also examines the frictions caused by heterogeneity in worker skills and employer demands, and studies the impact of other institutional structures. Personnel economics, which was largely developed in business schools, is the study of the employment relationship—particularly how firms or other employers can solve human resource management problems, given their broader strategic contexts (Oyer and Schaefer, 2011). It studies how firms should go about finding the right employees and frames this as an economic problem involving matching in the presence of search costs and bilateral asymmetric information.

41

Figure 4.1
Simplified View of the Labor Market for Cybersecurity
Professionals

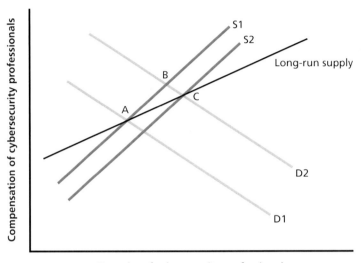

Quantity of cybersecurity professionals

RAND *RR430-4.1*

the demand for such professionals, met in such a way that there were few complaints that cybersecurity professionals could not be found, and the price paid for cybersecurity professionals overall was not terribly misaligned with the price paid for professionals with comparable education and skills. The intersection is illustrated by point A in Figure 4.1.

As discussed in Chapter One, the demand for cybersecurity professionals has risen sharply since 2007. This rise may be due to multiple factors, including increased connectivity, increased vulnerability, increased recognition by hackers of the value of attacking networks, and an increased awareness of hacking. In terms of Figure 4.1, these events pushed the demand curve to the right, from D1 to D2. The movement of the demand curve implies that—as we observe in today's market—many employers are willing to pay more to hire the same quality and type of professional they were hiring before 2007.

The rise in demand for cybersecurity has been fairly sudden. The curve of public concern over cybersecurity, which was rising in the early 1990s,[2] seems to have been suppressed after the Y2K non-crisis, the dot-com crash shortly thereafter, and the national reaction to the September 11th hijackings. The latter shifted attention from high-end threats (e.g., countries capable of conducting cyberwar) to low-end threats (e.g., terrorists). Then, the cybersecurity business awoke with a start circa 2007 with the Russian cyberattacks on Estonia and the brazen penetration of Pentagon computers by (putatively) Chinese hackers. The field has been on a tear ever since, focused on expanding manpower, with less demand for secure "mil-spec" technology from commercial vendors.

However, it takes time to develop more cybersecurity professionals in response to the heightened demand. Training and education can take years; even if individual workers in other occupations have the right set of skills to become cybersecurity professionals, they may not immediately switch occupations. Thus, in the short run, the supply curve for cybersecurity professionals is rather inelastic, or in other words, not very responsive to price. In terms of Figure 4.1, the sudden shift outward of the demand curve, from D1 to D2, leads to a movement along the short-run supply curve S1. The new equilibrium is at point B, which entails a substantial increase in compensation packages, with a relatively small increase in the number of cybersecurity professionals.

Point B can be viewed as a short-run equilibrium. In the longer term, the supply of cyberprofessionals is likely to shift outward for a variety of reasons. That is, there are likely to be more cyberprofessionals available at any given compensation level. As we noted in Chapter Three, a number of cybersecurity schools have been created, and organizations are actively training their employees in cybersecurity. Moreover, higher compensation packages in today's market are likely to attract more professionals from related fields, such as computer science and engineering, into the cybersecurity field. These factors are

---

[2] To be fair, the public apprehension about hacking preceded its actually happening to the systems owned by organizations (that is, those who had the resources to hire cybersecurity professionals to keep themselves safe).

represented in Figure 4.1 by an outward shift of the supply curve, from S1 to S2.

In the long run, the market should reach a new equilibrium at point C, where compensation is lower than it is in today's market, and the number of cybersecurity professionals is greater. Thus, the long-run supply curve for cybersecurity professionals passes through point A (the pre-2007 equilibrium point) and point C (the equilibrium point that will be reached after the increase in supply is realized). As shown in Figure 4.1, the long-run supply curve is likely to be more elastic (more responsive to price) than the short-run supply curves, because it is easier for people to move into and out of a profession in the longer term.

This simple view of the labor market for cybersecurity professionals is consistent with the empirical evidence of rising compensation witnessed in recent years. It also suggests that over time—barring any further increase in demand—the number of professionals will continue to increase, and compensation packages will begin to fall.

However, there are a number of factors that complicate the functioning of the labor market for cybersecurity professionals— particularly for government employers. In the next sections, we discuss these factors in more detail.

The Adjustment of Labor Demand to Shocks

The simplified view of the market for cybersecurity professionals discussed the fact that the supply of labor is likely to be fairly unresponsive in the short run. However, there is also a large literature analyzing the extent to which demand may also take time to adjust to an exogenous shock. The central insight of this literature is that there is a lag in the adjustment of labor demand to its long-run equilibrium because hiring and firing costs make full, immediate adjustment too costly (Nickell, 1986).

The term *hiring costs* applies to those costs generated over and above the wage payment when a new worker is hired. These costs may be due to time spent recruiting, vetting, and training (Oi, 1962).

The literature finds that hiring costs for skilled, professional, technical employees (such as cybersecurity professionals) are typically much larger than those for unskilled workers. One estimate is that such costs are 12 times as large (Rees, 1973).

The term *firing costs* applies to those costs generated by the release of an employee. Payments in lieu of notice, compensation for breach of contract, lost output due to lag between losing and replacing an employee, unemployment benefits, and compliance with labor laws regarding firing may all contribute to firing costs. Firing costs are typically higher for unionized workers and government employees than for private-sector workers.

Hiring and firing costs cause friction in the labor market and prevent firms from simply hiring and firing workers immediately in response to daily fluctuations in sales. Even when a firm has a strong expectation that demand for its output will increase over the following decade, it may be slow to hire new workers because it faces the risk that it will have to fire them if and when demand falls again. The costs of hiring and firing may exceed the marginal benefit of increased productivity due to a temporary increase in the workforce. There is considerable empirical evidence of such lags. One study on manufacturing, for example, finds that it takes at least a year for employment to adjust fully to a shift in sales (Sims, 1974).

According to the literature, adjustments in employment are particularly slow in more technical fields, like cybersecurity, which require high levels of education and training. There is a fairly sizable literature on the channels through which employers search for appropriate employees. One early contributor showed that employers can expand their searches by gathering more applications, by gathering more information on potential applicants, or both (Rees, 1966). In other words, they can expand their recruiting efforts or intensify their screening efforts.

A major empirical finding in this literature is that jobs that require more education or more training expenditures by the employer fill more slowly because employers spend more time on the search process. This is because an employer will want to ensure that the employee is a good match with a low probability of quitting before making costly investments in his or her training (Barron, Bishop, and Dunkelberg 1985). Our observation that training programs for new cybersecurity employees in government agencies are often long and intensive—up to three years at the NSA, for example—is therefore theoretically consistent with our observation that recruiting efforts are intensive and that hiring is expanding slowly. In terms of the simplified model discussed above, the relatively slow expansion of hiring suggests that the market is moving slowly from point A to point B. If the expansion is sufficiently slow relative to the influx of new cybersecurity personnel (in other words, the shift outward of the supply curve), then the market may never actually reach point B but rather may move along the path toward B, and then toward the long-run equilibrium. In that case, we would witness a rise in compensation packages, followed by a leveling off, rather than a decline.

Differences in Human Capital

The discussion above considered the supply of cybersecurity professionals as a whole. However, the market for cybersecurity professionals is very sensitive to differences in human capital. Broadly speaking, human capital can be defined as "any stock of knowledge or characteristics the worker has (either innate or acquired) that contributes to his or her 'productivity'" (Acemoglu and Autor, 2011). These characteristics may, for example, include years and quality of schooling, training, language aptitude, and attitudes toward work.

There are many different ways of thinking about human capital. The standard theory is that human capital increases a worker's productivity, and that it can therefore be viewed as an input in the production process (Becker, 1962). Another approach is to view human capital as the capacity to adapt to changing environments (Nelson and Phelps, 1966). A third view is that human capital is the capacity to fit into an organization, obey orders, and have the "correct" worldview (Bowles and Gintis, 1975). In all three views, acquiring human capital can be thought of as making an investment that has a financial return in the labor market.

The leading alternative view is that workers make costly human capital, not because it increases productivity, but because it can be used as a signal of higher quality when workers and employers have asymmetric information about the worker's competence for the job (Spence, 1973). Employers then offer wages conditional on the signal, which may be only weakly correlated with productivity.

Our interviews and literature review provided insight into some of the characteristics that government agencies use to identify human capital in potential cybersecurity hires. These include cybersecurity qualifications; a background in a technical subject like mathematics, physics, engineering, or computer science; innate technical talent; ability to become a skilled technician; interest in cybersecurity; participation in hackathons; U.S. citizenship; a security clearance; and qualities such as professionalism and ethics.

However, it is unclear which of these (or other) observable worker characteristics are actually associated with productivity, adaptability, and suitability in the cybersecurity context, and which are convenient signals or screening tools. Many of the desired characteristics are difficult to observe, which explains the comment frequently made by human resources staff that they struggle to tell the difference between good and bad candidates, and that cybersecurity credentials have proven to be only weakly correlated with competence. It also helps to explain why agencies use so many different mechanisms to screen cybersecurity applicants for quality. These include written job applications; interviews; certain observable characteristics listed above (cyber qualifications, academic background, hackathon participation, citizenship, security clearance); high performance on the DLAT; performance on basic ICT literacy tests; and internal recruiting and training.

The potential consequences of the difficulties of identifying applicant quality are highly dependent on what cybersecurity task is at issue. If the tasks are compliance, user interface issues, or trouble-ticket management, for instance, then the difference between mediocrity and excellence is likely to be tolerable, and the effort required to distinguish the two (over and above obvious but not necessarily accurate indicators such as education and certification) may not be worth the results. If the tasks, however, are forensics (e.g., finding evidence of APT attack), code-writing, or red-teaming, then the difference between mediocrity and excellence is likely to be very significant. As we discuss in more detail in the following chapter, it is the upper-tier professionals performing these latter tasks who are said to be the hardest to hire in today's labor market.

In the longer term, recruiting practices and selection criteria for cybersecurity professionals will likely become more refined and efficient as the cybersecurity career field becomes more mature and agencies accumulate more observations of how worker characteristics at the time of hiring relate to subsequent productivity. In addition, job matches typically improve over time for two reasons. First, while the productivity of a given employee/employer match is unknown at the time of hiring, it becomes known over time as the employer observes employee productivity. Good matches persist, whereas poor matches are terminated, so the average quality of matches within an organization improves over time, and the workforce becomes more stable (Jovanovic, 1979). The rate of separations decreases with job tenure.

A second reason that job matches improve over time is that employees gain organization-specific human capital as they receive more internal training and gain experience. As a result, employees become more valuable to their employers. As employees develop particular combinations of skills valued by their employers, it may become more costly for them to leave their jobs. They may have difficulty finding other jobs that demand and reward their particular basket of specialized skills (Lazear, 2009). So, employers also become more valuable to their employees.

Furthermore, over the long term, the organization can take advantage of its changing workforce more effectively by making other changes, such as capital investments or workplace reorganizations. Thus, the complementarity between the attributes of employers and employees can improve over time and lead to increases in productivity (Milgrom and Roberts, 1995).

Factors Related to Government Agency Characteristics

Under the human capital hypothesis, productivity—and, therefore, the wage structure—will largely be determined by human capital. Empirically, however, differences in schooling and other measures of human capital explain only a small portion of the variation in wages. Clearly, not all differences in pay are related to skills. Some of the observed differences in pay between government and private-sector cybersecurity professionals may be due to differences in skills, but there are other possible causes.

One alternative explanation is the use of compensating differentials. A worker may receive less monetary pay because she receives part of her compensation in terms of other job characteristics, some of which may be hard to observe (Rosen, 2004). These may include more pleasant working conditions; more interesting work; greater on-the-job learning; greater access to decisionmakers; greater prestige and recognition; job stability; reduced hours; lower effort requirements; better amenities; better benefits packages; more leave and vacation time; and better long-term promotion or career prospects. Working as a cybersecurity professional at a government agency, as opposed to a private company, may entail some or all of these benefits. It is conceivable that private-sector firms may have to offer workers a compensating wage differential to accept longer hours, less job stability, and less-attractive benefits.

Another explanation for wage differences is the presence of labor market imperfections or inefficiencies. Workers with the same human capital may be paid different wages because the jobs themselves—not the workers—differ in terms of their productivity. An important difference between government agencies and private companies is that government agencies have far less ability to reallocate the factors of production as they see fit. Budgets are approved by Congress annually, and agency leaders may have limited authority to raise additional funds, relocate their headquarters, close offices, fire workers easily, choose contractors, or make investment decisions at their own discretion. Jobs in government agencies may, therefore, be associated with lower productivity than comparable jobs in the private sector, because agencies have a long list of additional goals (other than productivity) to fulfill, plus many extra requirements and constraints. In particular, government agencies may have little control over their IT investments and workplace organization—two characteristics closely linked to overall productivity. Cybersecurity units of government agencies may, therefore, be less efficient than their private-sector counterparts, and so pay less.

Rules and regulations may be another source of variation in pay. Typically in the labor economics literature, demand for labor in some sector of the economy is thought to interact with the labor supply function to determine the level of wages. However, there is another body of literature that treats wage levels as being exogenous and analyzes how employment responds. This approach is often used to study highly unionized industries, where the wages employers offer must exceed some lower bound, or government agencies, where wages are constrained by fixed pay bands. The main finding of this literature is that relative wages affect the skill and age mixes of employees at given output, and that real wages affect the aggregate level of output and employment (Hamermesh, 1986).

These findings may help to explain the complaint that government agencies find it difficult to hire enough upper-tier cybersecurity professionals to meet their requirements. Economic theory suggests that an individual's labor supply is defined as the number of hours he is prepared to work, given the wage rate and the amount of non-labor income he has. In choosing what number of hours to work, an individual faces a trade-off between leisure and labor. Working more hours increases income but reduces the number of hours devoted to leisure.

Economists plot market labor supply curves by adding the quantity of labor supplied by each individual at each possible wage rate. A key implication of this procedure is that more individuals may be encouraged to enter the labor force as wages rise. Below some threshold level, no individual chooses to work. Above that threshold, one individual may choose to enter the labor force. Above a slightly higher threshold, a second worker may choose to enter the labor force, and so on.

In other words, an individual is modeled as being prepared to offer her labor to an employer, so long as the wage offered exceeds her reservation wage—or, in a more complex model, if the utility she would derive from the job exceeds her reservation utility. More skilled workers are modeled as having higher reservation wages or reservation utility levels.

To the extent that government wages are capped by federal wage schedules, the government must hire from the pool of workers willing to supply labor at the rates indicated in those schedules. Thus, pay bands may force government agencies to substitute toward younger, less experienced cybersecurity hires and away from older, more experienced professionals. Suppressed wages may also make workers inexpensive relative to capital and encourage employers to substitute away from capital and toward people, assuming there is some degree of substitutability.[3] We might therefore expect to see more young workers and fewer experienced workers in government agency cybersecurity units than in private-sector equivalents, as well as some effect on capital investments.

Although substituting toward younger, less-skilled workers may be one response to exogenous wages, it may not solve the government's hiring difficulties. Even if entry-level positions requiring fewer skills continue to make up the bulk of government cybersecurity hiring, the government may still have difficulty competing against private-sector employers, because of the nature of the payoffs from cybersecurity activities. The literature indicates that employers typically pay higher starting salaries and offer greater rewards for employee loyalty in fields where payoff distributions are highly variable (Andersson et al., 2009). One example in the literature is the video game industry, where a company can make millions of dollars if one of its programmers designs a popular game. Cybersecurity activities may similarly have widely varying payoffs, as one recent example of cybertheft illustrates. The recent data breach caused by a cyberattack against Target Corporation, Neiman Marcus, and other retailers will likely cost sev-

---

[3] If less-skilled cybersecurity workers and capital are complements, we may see an increase in both capital and less skilled workers.

eral billion dollars. Target alone will incur more than a billion dollars in costs, including $1.1 billion dollars in repayments to banks for fraudulent charges, and additional sums for lost sales, enhanced cybersecurity technologies, and compensation to shoppers (Langley, 2014). In the aftermath of this incident, retailers and other private sectors will likely be prepared to pay millions for cybersecurity expertise, and considerable sums even to entry-level employees.

A related aspect of the limits on government wages pertains to training. In a classic human capital model, training leads to higher productivity, which results in higher wages (Becker, 1962). Thus, workers reap the rewards of training, and the model suggests that workers—rather than firms—have an incentive to invest in training. However, when there are wage ceilings, firms are not able to fully reward workers for higher productivity, thus reducing the incentive for workers to make training investments themselves. As a result, employers with restrictive pay ceilings are predicted to bear a higher share of training costs. A related empirical result in the literature is that employers finance a greater portion of training costs when their skills requirements and training programs are more organization specific.

In government agency cybersecurity units, pay is capped, and training tends to be quite organization specific because the job typically involves becoming deeply familiar with the particular organization's computer systems. Both these characteristics are consistent with our finding that government agencies have predominantly hired entry-level cybersecurity staff with fewer qualifications but made substantial investments in internal recruitment and training.

Geographic Considerations

One finding in the personnel economics literature is that the location of an organization's recruitment efforts can have important effects on its workforce. Both the NSA and USCYBERCOM are located in Fort Meade, Maryland, and the CIA Headquarters is located in Langley, Virginia. Unsurprisingly, their outreach efforts into schools and universities and many of their recruiting efforts appear to be largely focused on the surrounding areas. This could plausibly lead to an increased concentration of cybersecurity schools and cybersecurity professionals in Maryland, Virginia, and Washington, D.C., in coming years.

The result could be what economists describe as a "thicker" local labor market. In thicker markets, there are reduced search costs and improved matches between firms and workers. Thicker labor markets are also associated with greater competition for labor, however, which could harm the government if private-sector companies are able to outbid them. The empirical literature suggests that thicker labor markets lead to higher productivity, greater wage inequality, and higher returns to skill (Wheeler, 2001) and to more assortative matching between "high quality" workers and "high quality" firms (Andersson, Burgess, and Lane, 2007).

As the local labor market for cybersecurity professionals in D.C., Maryland, and Virginia thickens, government agencies may face more pressure to improve their human resources packages. Alternatively, if they are unable to increase compensation, they may be required to cast their nets more widely and expand recruiting efforts across the country in places where the labor market for cybersecurity professionals is thinner, at the cost of more efficient matching.

Summary

The economics literature provides some insight into the trends witnessed in the market for cybersecurity professionals in recent years. A simple view of labor markets suggests that the sudden, rapid rise in demand would lead to substantial increases in compensation packages but relatively few new cybersecurity professionals, which is consistent with our findings from the literature reviews and interviews. In the longer term, as long as demand does not continue to rise, higher compensation packages, and increased efforts to train and educate people in cybersecurity, should increase the number of workers in the field, thus decreasing compensation packages. However, if demand continues to rise in the long run, then compensation packages may continue on their upward trend as well.

A number of complicating factors may make the short-run and long-run adjustments more challenging, particularly for government agencies. In the short run, employers may be slow to hire additional workers even when there is a shock to their demand, because of hiring and firing costs. In addition, government agencies may face difficulties in competing with private-sector firms, since government compensation packages are constrained by pay bands. The fact that government pay is constrained, and that many cybersecurity skills are agency specific, suggests that government agencies are likely to hire entry-level workers and invest in internal recruiting and training. This is consistent with the evidence from our interviews.

A related complicating factor is that it is often difficult to observe human capital before a worker is hired. Government agencies have developed a variety of screening tools to identify promising candidates, but it is not clear whether it is possible to identify certain key traits— such as innate ability—before hiring someone. The challenge is exacerbated for upper-tier cyberprofessionals hired to perform tasks such as forensics or code writing. In the next chapter, we discuss these upper-tier cyberprofessionals, who are said to be the hardest to hire in today's market.

CHAPTER FIVE

Upper-Tier Cybersecurity Professionals and Policy Options

This chapter has two parts. In the first, we address the usefulness of differentiating the market for upper-tier cybersecurity professionals, where the labor conditions are particularly tight, from the market for other cybersecurity professionals. In the second part, we explore approaches that may be considered and have been advocated as ways to address the current difficulty of finding qualified cybersecurity professionals.

The Search for the Upper-Tier Cybersecurity Professional

Even if the supply of most cybersecurity professionals can be satisfied by the systematic application of well-understood techniques for acquiring people and moving them through training, the same cannot be said for upper-tier cybersecurity professionals, of whom there is a much more serious shortfall, as argued by several studies (notably the CSIS study) and confirmed by many of the interviews (notably the NSA interview).

Who are the upper-tier cybersecurity professionals that people seem to be competing so hard for? More precisely, what differentiates them from the broader body of cybersecurity professionals? This is really two questions: What characteristic differentiates the upper tier from the middle tiers? and What percentage of the cybersecurity workforce consists of the upper tier?

According to our interviews, popular mythology suggests that these professionals have uncanny abilities to spot vulnerabilities or the subtle signs of penetration. Such experts are valuable, but they do not necessarily make up a high percentage of those that earn salaries that the government cannot compete for. Rather, the more valuable individuals are those who combine technical talent with business or organizational experience (which is typical of many other professions). In a sector in which people have to understand why it is important to be secure, even if security is a hassle and expensive to boot, people who can combine the technical and the managerial are best placed to guide security efforts from the inside or outside. Such necessary ancillary skills include the ability to manage groups of heterogeneous individuals, market the importance of security to others, and/or meld security considerations into the complex and multifaceted world of government decisionmaking. Such individuals are typically in their 30s, not 20s.

There is no fine dividing line between the upper tier and the rest, and attempts to find one in the statistics (e.g., by looking for a double-humped curve of population versus some parameter of quality) are doomed to failure. Descriptively, however, it appears that the upper tier is roughly the top few percent of the scale. As noted, Alan Paller refers to the distinction between frequent fliers and pilots—with the majority of the cybersecurity professionals in the former category and no more than a thousand in the latter category (adding that the country needed 10,000 in the latter category, but admitting there was little evidence that employers would actually hire these 10,000). An official of a large government employer of cybersecurity professionals argued that the total workforce of 600 were people that could be, with work, found and usefully tasked—but four individuals were identified as upper tier, and, under ideal conditions, that small corps could be tripled, but no further. Within an intelligence agency, the upper tier was defined at closer to the top ten percent.

One way to look at the distinction between the upper tier and the rest is in terms of government salary ranges. The average cybersecurity professional is compensated at the $80,000 per year range, while those who are members of "(ISC)2," average $100,000 per year; the latter tend to be more experienced and come with certifications.[1] Both averages are well within what the federal government can pay (as long as it is willing to be sufficiently flexible in terms of assigning grade and step levels; see also Dark Reading, 2013). However, once professionals can command more than $250,000 a year, the competitiveness of the U.S. government as an employer suffers correspondingly. One company we spoke with indicated that top cybersecurity professionals (not necessarily managers) can expect to earn $300,000 a year. At that range, government agencies have a hard time competing.

The NSA, given this problem, appears to do a credible job, in the sense that they can use the uniqueness of their mission to persuade their veterans to stay in the face of very large salary offers (typically, double—which then translates to near $300,000 a year). Those it loses are not necessarily lost from government service. Some of them recycle their skills with defense firms and other government contractors, but the government ends up paying twice as much for their services. Yet, in many cases, their skills go toward improving the security of the banking sector (which, from a strategic perspective on national security, is not necessarily a bad thing).

This suggests one potential dividing line between the upper tier and the rest: the dividing line between what the government can compete for (given what it can pay) and those that the government cannot compete for. When due account is made for the greater security of government service (although events such as the 2013 sequester certainly do not help make that argument), particularly vis-à-vis employers whose funding base is the up-and-down contracting business and the fact that those who work for contractors are expected to work more, sometimes much more, than 40 hours a week, an annual salary over $250,000 would seem to be the dividing line beyond which government employment is uncompetitive. Above that level can be found the

---

[1]   Data from Suby, 2013. The study adds that "more than 80 percent [of all information security professionals] had no change in employer or employment in the past year, and the number of professionals is projected to continuously grow more than 11 percent annually over the next five years" and goes on to observe that "56% of respondents believe there is a workforce shortage compared to 2% that believe there is a surplus" (p. 3).

few percentage points of the cybersecurity workforce whose requirements are hard to meet.

To the extent that the upper tier consists largely of those with experience, finding enough of them will take time. Were the problem, instead, one of finding bright young hackers, the policy thrust would be to identify these people accurately so that they might be hired or educated and directed into cybersecurity education/training prefatory to hiring. Their ranks can be increased within a few years (if such people have already started their undergraduate education, then the task is one of redirecting people from one career field to another). But if the problem is one of combining sufficient technical competence with sufficient experience, then it will take much longer to groom someone from technical promise to filling requirements so difficult to fill that those who can are rarely interested in working for the government directly, or, in some cases, indirectly. This is not to say that there are not faster techniques available. For instance, if jobs in the greatest demand require managerial experience, more intensive efforts can be made to take promising cybersecurity technicians, so to speak, and run them into management to determine more quickly which of them can achieve the rare combination of technical and managerial skills. But such a course can be costly, not only in temporarily thinning the ranks of the more technically adept, but in leaving them in low-level positions if they lack talent for management. Furthermore, this is something that cannot be very easily pushed from the outside by subsidizing more education or tax incentives.

Policy Options for Meeting Cybersecurity Needs

Apart from improving management in general, as the studies of Chapter Two have discussed, are there ways of filling cybersecurity needs faster? Several approaches may be offered, but there are reasons for tempering enthusiasm about each of them.

Recruit Early

If the U.S. need for upper-tier cybersecurity professionals were important enough, policymakers might think about a policy (often thought analogous to Israel's policy vis-à-vis fighter pilots)[2] in which people with a talent for cybersecurity would be channeled into that profession irrespective of their other talents (or preferences, for that matter). Nearly four in five STEM college students said they decided to study STEM in high school or earlier (78 percent). One in five (21 percent) decided in middle school or earlier (Microsoft, 2011). The growing importance of hackathons coupled with the media emphasis on cyberwar suggests that something like that may be under way.

Among those we interviewed, opinion was mixed on the value of holding hackathons. Two educators were skeptical: One offered that the participants were learning nothing new; another indicated that the notion that a multiplication of hackathons would solve the cybersecurity manpower problem was just not true. Three individuals, however, were quite enthusiastic about them. One runs them. Another would put hackathon stars through college with a government-funded scholarship, with no further questions asked (SFS, by contrast, requires getting a security clearance). Our assessment is that while these hackathons are not essential, they are both useful for highlighting the attractiveness of the cybersecurity profession (we read or heard nothing indicating that such contests overglamorize things) and inexpensive. They could usefully be held in currently underserved areas of the country (e.g., somewhere other than central Maryland).[3]

Our observation, admittedly based on two data points, is that the United States is a long way from where every potential hacker becomes a cybersecurity professional. Such a conclusion is based on the geographical concentrations that one finds in the cybersecurity business. In a world in which native talent is more or less evenly spread around

---

[2] There are indications that Israel, a country where most individuals must serve in the army, is starting to do the same with talented hackers (Bryant, 2013).

[3] Illinois is one example (IDES, 2013) and Virginia is another. See also Perlroth, 2013, and the Virginia Governor's Cup Cyber Challenge, a veritable smackdown of hacking for high school students that was the brainchild of Alan Paller and others in the field.

the country, one should not expect such regional disparities. Yet, in one Center of Academic Excellence, we found that a third of the students came from a catchment area that held only one percent of the nation's population. As noted, NSA has programs that concentrate its talent searches within high schools of the Baltimore and Washington metropolitan areas (and is reasonably satisfied with the results). A very back-of-the-envelope calculation suggests a full-court press throughout the country to find upper-tier cybersecurity specialists could increase the eligible labor force by an order of magnitude.

Alan Paller and others have argued in favor of an accelerated junior college curriculum that would graduate specialized cybersecurity professionals at an accelerated rate (Paller and Boggs, 2013). The new Cyber Student Initiative, which is part of the Secretary Honors Program announced last fall, is an attempt to engage community college students, including veterans, in cybersecurity work at DHS (Ballenstedt, 2013b). However, it is not clear that people with the intelligence to be good cybersecurity professionals would be satisfied tracking themselves into an educational path that ends short of a bachelor's degree. Emphasizing cybersecurity training vis-à-vis education would make sense if the requirement were urgent and temporary (as is the requirement for warfighters during a great war, when there is no tomorrow if the war is lost), or, conversely, the cybersecurity field is likely to present the same problems tomorrow as it does today. Neither is true. The cybersecurity field evolves particularly quickly. Not only is the interaction between measure (e.g., discovered vulnerabilities) and countermeasure (e.g., patches) very rapid, but key characteristics are also capable of evolving smartly. Fifteen years ago, offensive cyberoperations were dominated by the actions of the "wily hacker." Today, there is a great deal more emphasis on tool-making (e.g., malware creation). The skill sets for each are very different. Fifteen years from now (when junior college graduates would be in their mid-30s) the skill sets may be very different again.

Use Foreign Nationals

An initial approach to increasing the supply of cybersecurity professionals is to import them: e.g., by letting foreign students convert into immigrants via the H-1B program, through the L-1 visa for intra-company transfers, TN visas for Canadian or Mexican citizens, or by extension of the Optional Practical Training (OPT) program. These approaches are no panacea and might actually harm the goal of finding enough cybersecurity professionals to meet national security needs.

First, a great deal of cybersecurity work, particularly at the high end, is already internationalized. Examples include writing computer code or finding bugs in it (that is why companies such as Microsoft and Google have branch offices around the globe). Indeed, any problem that does not require hands-on testing can be shipped overseas if economics so dictates.

Second, security clearances are almost always required for government and related contractor employment. Foreigners are not citizens and typically cannot, therefore, get security clearances until, under the best of circumstances, five years have elapsed.[4] By joining the U.S. labor market, however, foreign nationals are likely to reduce the compensation premium of cybersecurity professionals, which may depress the numbers of native-born cybersecurity professionals willing to enter the field. While this reduction may be offset by the increase in foreign cybersecurity professionals, these individuals are unavailable for national security work. In the short run, suppressing non-cleared compensation levels may increase the relative attractiveness of cleared positions to cybersecurity professionals (thereby helping employers of cleared professionals). Yet it is unclear how quickly individuals can move between these two submarkets; gaining security clearance typically takes a year for citizens, and cybersecurity positions may be considered particularly sensitive and, hence, take longer to clear someone for.[5]

---

[4] This assumes the individual applies for citizenship as soon as possible, gets it immediately, and is the beneficiary of a clearance process that starts at least a year before citizenship is granted.

[5] The Edward Snowden affair is likely to exacerbate this lag time.

Differentiate Job Categories More Precisely

A recurrent issue in our discussions is the importance of recognizing the various distinctions between one and another subspecialty within the broader cybersecurity domain so that individuals can be more precisely identified for hire within these categories. Our respondents at the NSA, for instance, believe that a firm understanding of where to draw the lines, and what the task assignments and, hence, skill requirements are, is an important criterion in differentiating the more mature human-resources approach from the less mature approaches. They call for yet more precision in defining these various skill subspecialties and have lauded the contributions they have gotten from DHS's (aforementioned) NICE program. There appears to be a rough consensus on how many such sub-categories exist and how they are defined. The NSA, itself, defines roughly two dozen categories; its Ft. Meade neighbor, USCYBERCOM, defines 26 categories. NICE has 30 categories. One professor offered that there are a dozen categories—not really a contradiction if one is looking at the matter from the education rather than the occupational end.

How much more precision is needed? A lot depends on where one sits in the education-occupational cycle. Personnel bureaucracies use this type of information to develop skill maintenance/upgrade paths and set pay/perquisite levels. Differentiation is also important in deciding how many of what kind of people to give how much occupational training to—but such training times are usually measured in months rather than years.

Furthermore, if the government finds it difficult to hire only certain types of cybersecurity personnel, differentiation helps ensure that scarce resources for attracting talent are concentrated rather than spread around a much larger field. There appears to be a consensus, for instance, that system support/administration, compliance testing, and patch maintenance—to use three examples—are relatively easy-to-find skill sets. By contrast, people who understand what happens when "discrete network parameters, interfaces, data structures, and data standards" are changed, or who can write exploit or exploit-prevention code, are usually in shorter supply. So, it can be useful to have that level of differentiation—between those whom government agencies currently have in surplus and those they cannot easily find.

However, in dealing with the broad issue of moving the right individuals into the right programs to address the cybersecurity manpower problem, such differentiation may be unnecessary. There really is no set of unique predispositions among the career-choosers (or career-switchers) that suggests that placing someone with an aptitude for one subcategory (e.g., forensics) into another subcategory (e.g., code-testing) is harmful in comparison to letting people sort themselves out. True, organizations are leaning toward people with computer science degrees. Yet, there is little evidence to suggest that all upper-tier cyber-professionals will be found only in that profession. Several noted that deep curiosity and a drive to understand how things work are better predictors of top-notch cybersecurity capabilities than education credentials (much less professional credentials such as the CISSP). The Air Force observed that only half of its cyber weapons instructors even have STEM degrees.

The conclusion appears to be that while an efficient and accurate classification scheme is useful for managing cybersecurity professionals, its contribution to alleviating the current difficulty in finding enough good people should not be overstated. In theory, it would allow each job category to be filled separately and, thus, create a tighter match between vacancies and hires, thereby reducing the gross number of vacancies (since a surplus in one job category does not technically reduce the impact of a vacancy in another). In practice, these specialties really do not exist as distinct entities, and good cybersecurity people can be used in many related specialties.

Address Civil Service Issues

The conditions of civil service pose two types of barriers to retaining upper-tier cybersecurity professionals. One, as noted, is that salaries that top out at $150,000 (see Table 5.1) are uncompetitive for those who could otherwise command twice as much. The other, more subtle, consists of inflexibility in matching salaries. Federal agencies vary in this regard. The NSA, for instance, has considerable wage flexibility; not only can it offer premium wages in some cases, but it is not

Table 5.1
Annual Pay for Federal Cybersecurity Professionals, by Grade

Civilian Grade	Percentage of Occupation	Annual Pay Band ($)
GS-15	2	123,758–155,500
GS-14	12	105,211–136,771
GS-13	19	89,033–115,742
GS-12	28	74,872–97,333
GS-10/11	18	56,587–81,204
GS-8/9	17	46,745–67,114
GS-6/7	2	37,983–54,875
GS-5	2	34,075–44,293

SOURCES: Office of Personnel Management, 2012; occupational percentages from Department of Defense *Cyber Operations Personnel Report*, p. 15.

NOTE: Annual pay bands are for the Washington, D.C./Baltimore area.

uncommon, for instance, for a particularly clever technical expert to be paid at the GS-15 level while supervised by a GS-14. Other agencies such as the Air Force or DHS enjoy a good deal less flexibility.[6] One federal manager complained that while introductory pay scales sufficed to bring good people on board, the way that higher-level (GS-13 through GS-15) jobs are defined makes it difficult to promise that technically astute individuals could look forward to promotion based largely on their technical skills. Both problems—low ceilings and inflexibility—can be fixed, but it would cost money, test traditional civil service norms, and raise the dreaded "why him and not me ques-

---

[6] "The version [of the Senate cyber bill] authored by Sens. Joseph Lieberman (I-Conn.), Susan Collins (R-Maine) and Jay Rockefeller (D-W.Va.) calls for the National Cybersecurity and Communications Integration Center (NCCIC) to receive the same hiring authorities that the National Security Agency uses to recruit and retain critical employees. The bill allows the DHS secretary to establish positions in the excepted service, make direct appointments, set rates of basic pay and provide additional compensation, benefits, incentives and allowances" (Miller, 2012).

tion" among other professional specialties. However, there is a general authority within DoD to pay somewhat more to "highly qualified individuals," and creative use of the Intergovernment Personnel Act (IPA) can allow a few people to be brought into the federal government from outside without reducing the salary such individuals get for making the switch. Although more study may be necessary to validate the point, fixing the inflexibility may be more cost effective than simply raising the top pay scales.

Finally, the practice of paring back civil service hiring in favor of contractors, coupled with the relatively early ages at which federal employees can collect their pensions, means that a high percentage of cyberprofessionals who are civil servants are eligible to retire either now or over the next few years. Most such individuals are over 40, not only in the United States but in the United Kingdom.[7]

Review Veterans' Preferences

Veterans' preferences in federal hiring are another issue that may retard the federal government's ability to hire those it needs. Agency opinion on veterans' preference tends to be negative. Although those we talked to understood the importance of ensuring job opportunities for those who served, we heard at least one anecdote of a job opening that furnished three individuals, from whom the employer had to choose thanks to such preferences; none had cybersecurity experience (one was a shop owner). Conversely, another agency person opined that being a veteran was quite helpful if the cybersecurity position had a military context (which characterizes many national security positions). It certainly would not hurt if managers were trained on how to conduct a job search that meets their needs while complying with applicable laws.

---

[7] "'There are far too many people over 40 working in this area and not nearly enough in their twenties,' Baroness Pauline Neville-Jones told delegates at the ITEC conference in London yesterday" (Nguyen, 2012). See also Ballenstedt, 2013a: "The vast majority of the federal cybersecurity workforce is older than 40, an issue that could eventually lead to a personnel shortage in the field, according to a new report." And National Initiative for Cybersecurity Education and Federal Chief Information Officer's Council, 2013, found that nearly 80 percent of federal cybersecurity workers are over the age of 40, with most being closer to the retirement age threshold. Only 5 percent of the federal cyber workforce is 30 years of age or younger, the study found.

As with many such policies, veterans' preferences come with a price, but it is not a price unique to the cybersecurity field—or one that could not be overcome by sufficient precision in specifying the minimum qualifications needed for the field.

Use Guard and Reserve Units

The case for using Guard and Reserve units to address the shortfall in cybersecurity manpower is ostensibly compelling. It allows people to serve the national defense in emergencies, while keeping their civilian jobs (and the high salaries they pay). Individuals in such units would be current both with military perspectives on cybersecurity (thanks to their training) and with trends within the broader commercial sector. Proponents speak highly of the National Guard's 262nd Network Warfare Squadron, whose ranks include employees from Microsoft and other Puget Sound high-technology companies (Applegate, forthcoming).

Notwithstanding the good work such units can do, several considerations should be noted before pressing this as a key policy to address cybersecurity manpower issues. One is that it might address the military's need for cybersecurity at the expense of the rest of the economy's needs in a crisis. Second, to the extent that defending a system requires knowledge of the system being defended, such units still have to climb the local learning curve, once deployed, to offer useful contributions. Third, to the extent that it is in the nature of *offensive* cyberspace operations that they take long to prepare but need to be discharged at the outset of conflict (while the defender has yet to switch to wartime operational security modes, and before the effect wears off or is reversed), there are limits to the kind of help that an outside group can offer while coming up to speed. The infiltration that allows a cyberattack to take place happens before any such crisis begins. Conversely, if cyberattacks are severe enough to knock out communications entirely, such units can re-create communications infrastructure using technologies such as very small-aperture satellite terminals under auspices of Defense Support to Civil Authorities.

Outsource More

If the federal/military market cannot compete with the private market for cybersecurity professionals, why not join it? To a large extent, they have already merged. From the public policy perspective, a key question is whether what remains in the federal/military market is irreducibly limited to federal/military jobholders or whether further outsourcing is possible and wise. Note that outsourcing essentially shifts the challenges to the government from those involving long vacancies and underqualified applicants to others involving high salary costs plus the challenges of contracting and working with less-permanent labor.

Reducing the Demand for Cybersecurity Professionals

Another approach to meeting cybersecurity manpower needs, one that addresses issues that we did not raise in our interviews, is to reduce the global demand for such individuals. Admittedly, none of our interviewees took that tack, in all likelihood because their job was dealing with increasing supply (or smoothing the fit between supply and demand). Yet, there are options that may be worth pursuing.

The most obvious way to reduce the demand for cybersecurity manpower is to make cyberspace a safer place[8] (downplaying the problem will also reduce demand, but this is not recommended). There are many global approaches, such as increasing the resources put to prosecuting cybercrime, or adopting a serious deterrence strategy,[9] but it takes *additional* cybersecurity professionals (e.g., for forensics, attribution,

---

[8] Obvious does not mean correct, however, unless one believes that those who hire cybersecurity professionals are satisficers rather than optimizers. Satisficers will hire until the remaining cybersecurity problem is below some threshold. Optimizers will hire until the contribution of the next cybersecurity professional is less than what it costs to employ the individual. One can imagine tools (e.g., better anomaly indicators) that would reduce the overall insecurity of the network while increasing the productivity of individual cybersecurity professionals. A satisficer would pocket the gains and stop hiring cybersecurity professionals until insecurity rose above some threshold. An optimizer would employ more newly empowered cybersecurity professionals.

[9] Serious basically means declared red lines that countries are willing to act on in the face of risks that matters may escalate or that the accused state is, in fact, innocent.

offensive cyber operations) to be used in suppressing before the harvest of greater cybersecurity can be reaped. Only then can system owners, themselves, start to reduce their demand for cybersecurity professionals.

Alternatively, system owners could employ more attack-resistant architectures. One that has the prominent support of General Keith Alexander (then Director of the NSA) is to couple a thin-client architecture with cloud-based services; in essence, as much of the processing as possible would be done centrally rather than locally. This has two advantages. First, the thinner the client, the smaller its attack surface, and therefore the harder it is to attack it. Second, centralizing services within clouds permits economies of scale in securing systems; cloud providers can specialize in security, thereby reducing the demand made on individual system owners to secure their systems.

Abjuring certain applications or lightening up those that cannot be avoided is another approach. By far the greatest current source of breached systems undertaken for the purposes of installing persistent malware arises from vulnerabilities in Java (more broadly, from cross-site scripting) and Adobe products (notably Flash Player), both of which can be replaced for office work. Although the ".pdf" file is hard to replace, there are open-source ".pdf" readers that can read most such documents without invoking problematic code buried in these documents.[10] More operational options such as employing least-privilege architectures, and using whitelisting to limit what systems install, can reduce the incidence or severity of attack and replace upper-tier cybersecurity professionals (who hunt for APT attacks) with more ordinary professionals as required to enforce compliance with such options. More broadly, the federal/military demand for such professionals could benefit from stepping back and determining what strategy could minimize the expected combined loss from cybersecurity incidents plus the cost of incident prevention/management. The practical work of defin-

---

[10] "In the past, Foxit Reader has been suggested by some people in the security community as a more secure and less attacked alternative to Adobe Reader. In fact, Foxit, the company that develops the application, claims on its website that Foxit Reader is 'the most secure PDF reader' and is 'better than Adobe PDF Reader and Acrobat.'" That noted, the title of the article from which the quote is taken suggests that it is not completely free of flaws (Constantin, 2013).

ing this option requires determining what additional cybersecurity manpower would be asked to do, and assessing how badly such tasks need to be done.

A variant on that approach is to use more malware-resistant clients. PC architectures (including Mac-OS machines) were designed to make it very easy to alter the instruction sets that run on them. Cell phone (and tablet) architectures make it much more difficult and are, as a result, more secure in general (despite hand-wringing over bring-your-own-devices to work). One operating system, having been installed in almost a billion devices, has yet to attract malware in any significant way—although it is falls short of being *provably* secure.

A more fundamental shift is to migrate to clients whose instruction set is fixed (say, burned into the hardware). A former Microsoft executive has suggested that a machine with its operating system, web browser, office automation suite, and some network management tools in hardware would satisfy the needs of 90 percent of all office workers and would be provably safe from malware (once turned off and back on). Granted, this would not make it provably secure because there are many forms of attack that do not rely on malware (e.g., user and session hijacking, Structured Query Language injection attacks on databases). More importantly, such a machine would not be able to absorb new software or fix bugs in existing software very easily. But there is no technical reason that organizations cannot make such trade-offs if they perceive that the cost of insecurity is unaffordable or that the cybersecurity manpower required to achieve an adequate level of security is unavailable.

CHAPTER SIX

Conclusions

Early in our work we discovered that there was a broad consensus on a perceived shortage of cybersecurity professionals. The argument goes as follows. Everyone wants better protectors in cyberspace. Good people are snapped up quickly, and the best people tend to jump from employer to employer, with each move bringing an upward ratchet in compensation. As a result, the national security establishment in particular, and the country—perhaps world—as a whole is far more vulnerable to cyberattack than it thinks it should be. This is a crisis that requires an urgent remedy.

Our assessment does not refute this position—good cybersecurity professionals *are* in high demand—but it suggests these fears be tempered, that many forces are at work to fix the situation, and that the case for additional effort beyond that is not particularly strong. With the caveat that the statistics on the nascent cybersecurity profession are far from definitive, we nevertheless offer the following observations.

First, whenever rapid demand increases hit a profession with non-trivial skill and/or education requirements, economic theory suggests that rapidly rising compensation packages and strong competition for workers can be expected. When contemplating future increases either budgeted (e.g., expanding USCYBERCOM) or notional (e.g., hiring enough cybersecurity professionals to secure the critical infrastructure), it looks as though a severe crisis exists because the additional manpower to fill new billets cannot be identified given historical compensation levels.

Second, in response to earlier indications of burgeoning demand for cybersecurity professionals, there has already been a large increase in education, notably government-supported education, but also an increase in the number of computer science majors. These initiatives include Centers of Academic Excellence, scholarships for service, and support for skills updating. Similarly, a growing number of programs and contests (hackathons) have been created to identify promising young hackers.

Third, theory suggests and experience confirms that the market may take a long time to respond to unexpected increases in demand. In the short term, private employers are likely to address higher manpower demands by paying higher wages. We are also likely to observe vacancies staying unfilled for longer times, and employees moving more rapidly between organizations. Government agencies face a more difficult challenge, since their pay scales are constrained; they may therefore focus on hiring entry-level employees and training them. In the longer term, higher compensation packages, as well as the many education and training programs for cybersecurity that have recently been developed, should attract more qualified individuals to the profession, thus increasing supply and reducing wages to some extent. Because fundamental career choices are often made at the high school level or earlier, it could take a number of years for the consequences of the increased education and training to be realized. The late 1990s (the dot-com era) produced an earlier boom in information technology career choices, but by the time those inspired to pursue that field graduated (circa 2004) the market was considerably less attractive than it earlier seemed.

Fourth, in the short term, many large organizations have found innovative ways of meeting the demand for cybersecurity professionals through internal recruitment and training, as our interviews have found. Fortunately, the correlation between educational credentials and proven skill at enhancing cybersecurity is loose enough that talented individuals with non-IT training can be identified through testing and evaluation for traits such as curiosity and persistence. These individuals can then be trained for periods ranging from several months to a few years and then find useful employment solving cybersecurity manpower supply problems. As a result, such organizations rarely have to bid for individuals, so to speak, from external labor markets.

Fifth, theory suggests and our interviews confirm that even organizations that can meet most of their needs internally still face difficulties in recruiting or retaining cybersecurity professionals in the upper tier. The upper tier can be defined as those the top few percent of the cybersecurity profession or those people capable of commanding salaries of $200,000–$250,000 a year or more, and, importantly for our purposes, significantly beyond what the government can pay. Contrary to initial impressions, the top tier is not necessarily composed of young geniuses so much as those who possess the right combination of technical talents and organizational experience (notably administrative, managerial, bureaucratic, and/or marketing smarts). Typically, they tend to be in their 30s (or older), not their 20s. The experience factor suggests that it will take longer for supply to increase for the upper tier than for the rest of the profession. In terms of attracting potential upper-tier cybersecurity professionals, increasing training capacity does not seem to be as effective (there is little evidence that good people cannot get training) as do initiatives to attract them into the cybersecurity profession in the first place.

This, then, leads to our primary conclusion: the difficulty in finding qualified cybersecurity candidates is likely to solve itself, as the supply of cyberprofessionals currently in the educational pipeline increases, and the market reaches a stable, long-run equilibrium. This equilibrium may take some time to achieve. This does not mean that organizations will necessarily feel that they can find "enough" cyberprofessionals at an "affordable" price; the equilibrium is likely to feature compensation packages that are lower than today's packages but higher than they were prior to, say, 2007. Current efforts—in education, awareness, and job classifications—should be continued, but it is unlikely that major new initiatives are needed to help the market stabilize in the long run. It would also be helpful to be alert to the possibility of overdoing existing programs if indications of a decrease in the demand for cybersecurity professionals started to appear.

That noted, we have a few modest recommendations to offer. These recommendations are based on meeting needs as perceived by government and business.

Civil service and related rules that unnecessarily prevent federal agencies from hiring talented cybersecurity professionals should be waived for such hires. At a minimum, NSA's ability to waive the rules should be extended to all. It is also important to maintain government hiring of cybersecurity professionals through events such as sequestrations.

A modest infusion of funds (perhaps matching funds) should go to cybersecurity education programs to allow them to buy the necessary software licenses and computing/network equipment for their students.[1]

There are deliberate efforts to refine testing to identify candidates likely to succeed in cybersecurity careers. The Air Force now uses an aptitude test that is not based solely on prior STEM education, and the joint community is reworking the Armed Services Vocational Aptitude Battery to also serve this purpose. R&D should be invested in refining the testing instruments used to assess an innate ability to learn and understand the cyber domain and the nuances of information manipulation or protection.[2]

Lastly, and taking a longer perspective, more methods to attract women into this profession may also increase long-term supply. Although only a quarter of all STEM professionals are women, the percentage of women within the upper tier of the cybersecurity profession is well within single digits (Beede et al., 2011).

---

[1] This may have the side benefit of increasing the rate at which vulnerabilities in such software and hardware are found and reported so they may be fixed, improving cybersecurity for all future users.

[2] There are several examples of techniques in use today: personal interviews to assess the curiosity of the applicant to understand what's going on behind the video game—and ability to manipulate the game, sequential aptitude testing to identify the top one-third of progressing cyber classes and find unanticipated talent, or throwing the varsity players into the pool and allowing the competitive nature to drive their results.

In the Longer Run

Nothing about cyberspace stands still, and it is unlikely that the demand for cybersecurity professionals will stay constant at today's level. Typically, observers believe that demand will rise rather than fall; if so, then a return to long-run labor-market equilibrium may well be a slower process. The primary recommendation in this report to let events take their course, in that case, may well have been in error. Conversely, if it turns out that the current demand for cybersecurity workers contains an element of hyperbole, then even today's efforts to induce people to specialize in cybersecurity and educate themselves thusly may appear foolish, hobbling the careers of many people who would be an asset in other professions.

Labor markets do have ways of surprising people who have invested themselves in them. Consider the fate of someone born in 1945, whose first serious exposure to world events was Russia's Sputnik launch. This achievement stoked fears that the United States was falling behind in science—and thus needed to produce more scientists and engineers, urgently. Such an event would have taken place early in this person's seventh grade. So inspired, this individual leans heavily into a math and science focus in high school (graduating in 1963), and majors in aeronautical engineering (circa 1967) as the Apollo program is getting into high gear. As this person is smart and ambitious, a master's degree in engineering (circa 1969) is also sought and achieved. The future of someone who answered the country's call looked promising. Yet, by the early 1970s, the era of endless growth came to a shuddering end; many layoffs ensued. Had this individual stayed the course over an entire career, there would have been ups (e.g., the 1980s) and downs, and it all may have ended well, but not nearly as well as it looked when the educational commitments were made. A similar story could be told of nuclear scientists and engineers, the future demand for which was supposed to be unlimited—until nuclear power, once forecast to be "too cheap to meter," proved less popular than hoped.

Might cybersecurity suffer the same fate—with the young induced to learn its skills only to find that when the time comes to employ them, they aren't needed? On the one hand, this seems unlikely. The demand for aerospace engineers was created by the demand for aerospace products and services, which was externally driven: The government pushed, then politics changed (the moon was conquered and the Vietnam War peaked) and the government pulled back. The demand for cybersecurity professionals is driven by external circumstances (e.g., crime, the advanced persistent threat, and the growth of and dependence on networking), though government interest in the field is also a major driver. As long as the threat exists, there would seem to be sufficient demand for cybersecurity services.

The truth of that statement, however, depends on how long the current systems architecture stays in place (as was discussed at the end of the previous chapter). Many cybersecurity problems and most of the serious cybersecurity problems arise when hackers can insert rogue instructions into machines—otherwise known as malware. The elimination of malware would not lead to perfect cybersecurity. Indeed, most cybersecurity incidents arise from everyday omissions in authentication protocols and the like. But incidents that do not involve malware can generally be handled by completing what one aerospace executive we talked to termed the "80 percent problem" of ensuring that computer users practice good hygiene; for example, following guidance to avoid opening links in suspicious email or responding to unsolicited requests for personal information or passwords. It does not take an upper-tier cybersecurity person to carry out that kind of administrative housework, and, as noted, organizations are not having serious difficulties finding people outside that upper tier.

Malware is different, though. It requires systems that can accept changes to their instructions, largely by means that bypass user controls. Malware is a change harmful to the user's interests, but the fact that such changes are at all possible is a feature of computers that, at least until recently, has not been a feature of equally complex and dynamic products (e.g., cars, cameras). Such a feature has its benefits; it allows systems to run a limitless variety of programs, but it comes with costs. If the cybersecurity problem is truly getting worse and thereby demands the services of increasingly expensive professionals, might not the rising cost of using today's architecture increasingly cause people to question its dominance?

Therein lies a paradox for the cybersecurity profession. At first glance, how could demand not rise? Computers are growing more ubiquitous, particularly as equipment of all sorts (e.g., the automobile) keeps getting digitized and networked. Software is more complex, thereby increasing the attack surface. New devices, computers, and network applications come with new vulnerabilities, largely because convenience is valued more highly than security and resilience. The threats are growing smarter, and new threat actors are learning that they can attack the United States in cyberspace when any other form of assault is impossible. Yet, the more expensive and knotty is the cyberthreat, the greater the odds that the target may turn to radically new technology and architectures, which can sharply reduce the harm that threats can cause, and with it the need for so many talented cybersecurity professionals.

References

Acemoglu, Daron, and David Autor, *Lectures in Labor Economics,* manuscript, Massachussetts Institute of Technology Department of Economics, 2011.

Alexander, Gen. Keith B., statement before the Senate Committee on Armed Services, March 12, 2013.

Andersson, Fredrik, Simon Burgess, and Julia I. Lane, "Cities, Matching and the Productivity Gains of Agglomeration," *Journal of Urban Economics,* Vol. 61, No. 1, February 2007, pp. 112–128.

Andersson, Fredrik, Matthew Freedman, John Haltiwanger, Julia Lane, and Kathryn Shaw, "Reaching for the Stars: Who Pays for Talent in Innovative Industries?" *Economic Journal,* Vol. 119, June 2009, pp. F308-F332.

Applegate, Scott, "Leveraging Cyber Militias as a Force Multiplier in Cyber Operations," Carlisle, Pa.: U.S. Army War College, Strategic Studies Institute, forthcoming.

Assante, Michael J., and David H. Tobey, "Enhancing the Cybersecurity Workforce," *ITProfessional,* January/February 2011, Vol. 13, No. 1, pp. 12-15.

Ballenstedt, Brittany, "Report Warns of Potential Brain Drain in Federal Cyber Force," *Nextgov,* April 4, 2013a. As of April 30, 2014:
http://www.nextgov.com/cio-briefing/wired-workplace/2013/04/report-identifies-potential-brain-drain-federal-cyber-force/62296/

———, "DHS Creates Cyber Internships for Community College Students, Veterans," *Nextgov,* April 22, 2013b. As of April 30, 2014:
http://www.nextgov.com/cio-briefing/wired-workplace/2013/04/dhs-creates-cyber-internships-community-college-students-veterans/62680/

Barron, John M., John Bishop, and William C. Dunkelberg, "Employer Search: The Interviewing and Hiring of New Employees," *Review of Economics and Statistics,* Vol. 67, 1985, pp. 43–52.

Becker, Gary S., "Investment in Human Capital: A Theoretical Analysis," *Journal of Political Economy,* Vol. 70, No. 5, Part 2, October 1962, pp. 9-49.

Beede, David, Tiffany Julian, David Langdon, George McKittrick, Beethika
Khan, and Mark Doms, *Women in STEM: A Gender Gap to Innovation,*
U.S. Department of Commerce, ESA Issue Brief #04-11, August 2011. As of
April 30, 2014: http://www.esa.doc.gov/Reports/
women-stem-gender-gap-innovation

Bowles, Samuel, and Herbert Gintis, "The Problem with Human Capital
Theory—A Marxian Critique," *American Economic Review: Papers and Proceedings,*
Vol. 65, No. 2, May 1975, pp. 74-82.

Brannigan, Martha, "As Cyberthreats Rise, Army and Others Seek a Few Good
Hackers," *Miami Herald,* October 31, 2012, p. 1B.

Brown, Robbie, "Hacking of Tax Records Has Put States on Guard," *New York
Times,* November 5, 2012. As of April 29, 2014:
http://www.nytimes.com/2012/11/06/us/south-carolina-tax-hacking-puts-other-
states-on-alert.html

Bryant, Christa Case, "Israel Accelerates Cybersecurity Know-How as Early as
10th Grade," *Christian Science Monitor,* June 9, 2013. As of April 30, 2014:
http://www.csmonitor.com/World/Middle-East/2013/0609/
Israel-accelerates-cybersecurity-know-how-as-early-as-10th-grade

Constantin, Lucian, "Foxit Reader Security Flaw Reportedly Allows Attack,"
PCWorld, January 13, 2013. As of April 30, 2014:
http://www.pcworld.com/article/2025154/foxit-reader-security-flaw-reportedly-
allows-attack.html

Dark Reading, "California and Metro Washington D.C.—Top Destinations for
Cyber Security Talent: Cyber Security Professionals Looking for Employers with
Code of Honor; Report Average Salaries of $116,000," *InformationWeek,* August 5,
2013. As of April 30, 2014:
http://www.darkreading.com/california-and-metro-washington-dc-and-8211-top-
destinations-for-cyber-security-talent/d/d-id/1140244?

Davidson, Joe, "NSA to Cut 90 Percent of Systems Administrators," *Washington
Post,* August 13, 2013. As of April 30, 2014:
http://www.washingtonpost.com/blogs/federal-eye/wp/2013/08/13/
nsa-to-cut-90-percent-of-systems-administrators/

Evans, Karen, and Franklin Reeder, "A Human Capital Crisis in Cybersecurity:
Technical Proficiency Matters," CSIS Commission on Cybersecurity for the
44th Presidency, Center for Strategic and International Studies, November 2010.

Fulghum, David, "Solitary Genius Trumped by the Socially Adept," *Aviation Week
and Space Technology,* July 30, 2012, p. 32.

GAO—*See* U.S. Government Accountability Office.

Gjelten, Tom, "Cyberwarrior Shortage Threatens U.S. Security," NPR News, July 19, 2010. As of April 29, 2014:
http://www.npr.org/templates/story/story.php?storyId=128574055

Hamermesh, Daniel S. "The Demand for Labor in the Long Run," in Orley Ashenfelter and Richard Layard, eds., *Handbook of Labor Economics, Vol. 1,* Amsterdam: Elsevier Science Publishers, 1986, pp. 429-471.

Hollis, David M., "A Reserve Component Initiative to Defend DoD and National Cyberspace," *Small Wars Journal,* Small Wars Foundation, November 10, 2011.

Homeland Security Advisory Council, *CyberSkills Task Force Report,* U.S. Department of Homeland Security, Fall 2012.

Hutchins, Eric M., Michael J. Clopperty, and Rohan M. Amin, "Intelligence-Driven Computer Network Defense Informed by Analysis of Adversary Campaigns and Intrusion Kill Chains," Lockheed Martin Corporation, November 21, 2010. As of April 29, 2014:
http://www.ciosummits.com/LM-White-Paper-Intel-Driven-Defense.pdf

Identity Theft Resource Center, "ITRC 2013 Breach List Tops 600 in 2013," 2013. As of April 29, 2014:
http://www.idtheftcenter.org/ITRC-Surveys-Studies/2013-data-breaches.html

Illinois Department of Employment Security, "Governor Quinn Launches Cyber Challenge," press release, April 1, 2013. As of April 30, 2014:
http://www.ides.illinois.gov/Lists/News%20and%20Announcements/DispForm.aspx?ID=67

Jovanovic, Boyan, "Job Matching and the Theory of Turnover," *Journal of Political Economy,* Vol. 87, No. 5, Part 1, October 1979, pp. 972–990.

Langley, Monica, "Inside Target, CEO Gregg Steinhafel Struggles to Contain Giant Cybertheft," *Wall Street Journal,* February 18, 2014.

Lazear, Edward P., "Firm-Specific Human Capital: A Skill-Weights Approach," *Journal of Political Economy,* Vol. 117, No. 5, October 2009, pp. 914–940.

Lord, Kristin M., and Jacob Stokes, "Help Wanted: Geek Squads for US Cybersecurity," *Christian Science Monitor,* August 8, 2012. As of April 29, 2014:
http://www.csmonitor.com/Commentary/Opinion/2012/0808/Help-wanted-Geek-squads-for-US-cybersecurity

Mandiant, *APT 1: Exposing One of China's Cyber Espionage Units,* Alexandria, Va., February 2013. As of April 29, 2014:
http://intelreport.mandiant.com

Microsoft Corporation, "Microsoft Releases National Survey Findings on How to Inspire the Next Generation of Doctors, Scientists, Software Developers and Engineers," press release, September 7, 2011. As of April 30, 2014:
http://www.microsoft.com/en-us/news/press/2011/sep11/09-07msstemsurveypr.aspx

Milgrom, Paul, and John Roberts, "Complementarities and Fit: Strategy, Structure, and Organizational Change in Manufacturing," Journal of Accounting and Economics, Vol. 19, Nos. 2–3, March–May 1995, pp. 179–208.

Miller, Jason, "Napolitano Wants NSA-Like Hiring Authority for DHS Cyber Workforce," Federal News Radio, October 31, 2012. As of April 30, 2014:
http://www.federalnewsradio.com/473/3101703/
Napolitano-wants-NSA-like-hiring-authority-for-DHS-cyber-workforce

Morse, Amyas, The UK Cyber Security Strategy: Landscape Review, National Audit Office, HC 890, London: The Stationery Office, February 2013.

Nakashima, Ellen, and Brian Krebs, "As Attacks Increase, U.S. Struggles to Recruit Computer Security Experts," Washington Post, December 23, 2009. As of April 29, 2014:
http://www.washingtonpost.com/wp-dyn/content/article/2009/12/22/
AR2009122203789.html

National Initiative for Cybersecurity Education and Federal Chief Information Officer's Council, 2012 Information Technology Workforce Assessment for Cybersecurity (ITWAC) Summary Report, Department of Homeland Security, March 14, 2013. As of April 30, 2014:
https://cio.gov/wp-content/uploads/downloads/2013/04/ITWAC-Summary-Report_04-01-2013.pdf

Nelson, Richard R., and Edmund S. Phelps, "Investment in Humans, Technological Diffusion, and Economic Growth," American Economic Review, Vol. 56, No. 1/2, March 1966, pp. 69–75.

Nguyen, Anh, "UK Cybersecurity Professionals Are 'Too Old,' Says Baroness Neville-Jones," Computerworld UK, May 24, 2012. As of April 30, 2014:
http://www.computerworlduk.com/news/careers/3359837/
uk-cybersecurity-professionals-are-too-old-says-baroness-neville-jones/

Nickell, S. J., "Dynamic Models of Labour Demand," in Orley Ashenfelter and Richard Layard, eds., Handbook of Labor Economics, Vol. 1, Amsterdam: Elsevier Science Publishers, 1986.

Office of Personnel Management, Salary Table 2012-DCB, January 2012. As of April 30, 2014:
https://www.opm.gov/policy-data-oversight/pay-leave/salaries-wages/2012/
general-schedule/dcb.pdf

Oi, Walter Y. "Labor as a Quasi-Fixed Factor," Journal of Political Economy, Vol. 70, No. 6, December 1962, pp. 538–555.

Open Security Foundation, Data Loss Database, undated. As of April 29, 2014:
http://datalossdb.org/statistics

Oyer, Paul, and Scott Schaefer, "Personnel Economics: Hiring and Incentives," in O. Ashenfelter and D. Card, eds., Handbook of Labor Economics, Edition 1, Vol. 4, No. 5, Amsterdam: Elsevier, 2011.

Ozment, Andy, and Stuart Schechter, "Milk or Wine: Does Software Security Improve with Age?" 15th USENIX Association Security Symposium, Proceedings, 2006, pp. 93–104. As of April 29, 2014:
http://research.microsoft.com/pubs/79177/milkorwine.pdf

Paller, Alan, and George Boggs, "Why We Need More Troops for Escalating Cyberwar," USA Today, March 29, 2013. As of April 30, 2014:
http://www.usatoday.com/story/tech/2013/03/28/
cyberwar-obama-executive-order-training-troops/2029309/

Partnership for Public Service and Booz Allen Hamilton, "Cyber IN-Security: Strengthening the Federal Cybersecurity Workforce," Partnership for Public Service, July 22, 2009.

Perlroth, Nicole, "Luring Young Web Warriors is Priority. It's Also a Game," New York Times, March 24, 2013. As of April 30, 2014:
http://www.nytimes.com/2013/03/25/technology/united-states-wants-to-attract-hackers-to-public-sector.html

Rastello, Sandrine, and Jeanna Smialek, "Cybersecurity Starts in High School with Tomorrow's Hires," Bloomberg News, May 16, 2013. As of April 29, 2014:
http://www.bloomberg.com/news/2013-05-16/cybersecurity-starts-in-high-school-with-tomorrow-s-hires.html

Rees, Albert, "Information Networks in Labor Markets," American Economic Review, Papers and Proceedings, Vol. 56, No. 2, 1966, pp. 559–566.

———, The Economics of Work and Pay, New York: Harper and Row, 1973.

Rosen, Sherwin, Markets and Diversity. Cambridge, Mass.: Harvard University Press, 2004.

Rosenblatt, Seth, "Ten-Year-Old Hacker Finds Zero-Day Flaw in Games," CNET, Download Blog, August 7, 2011. As of April 29, 2014:
http://download.cnet.com/8301-2007_4-20089152-12/10-year-old-hacker-finds-zero-day-flaw-in-games/

Salzman, Hal, Daniel Kuehn, and B. Lindsay Lowell, Guestworkers in the High-Skill U.S. Labor Market: An Analysis of Supply, Employment, and Wage Trends, Washington, D.C.: Economic Policy Institute, April 24, 2013.

Scott, Lynn M., Raymond E. Conley, Richard Mesic, Edward O'Connell, and Darren D. Medlin, Human Capital Management for the USAF Cyber Force, Santa Monica, Calif.: RAND Corporation, DB-579-AF, 2010. As of April 29, 2014:
http://www.rand.org/pubs/documented_briefings/DB579.html

Sims, Christopher A., "Output and Labor Input in Manufacturing," Brookings Papers on Economic Activity, Vol. 3, 1974.

Spence, Michael A., "Job Market Signaling," *Quarterly Journal of Economics,* Vol. 87, No. 3, August 1973, pp. 355–374.

Starr, Stu, Daniel Kuehl, and Terry Pudas, "Perspectives on Building a Cyber Force Structure," Conference on Cyber Conflict Proceedings 2010, Talinn, Estonia: CCD COE Publications, 2010.

Suby, Michael, *The 2013 (ISC)2 Global Information Security Workforce Study,* Frost & Sullivan and Booz Allen Hamilton, 2013. As of April 30, 2014: https://www.isc2.org/GISWSRSA2013/

U.S. Department of Defense, *Cyber Operations Personnel Report,* Report to Congressional Defense Committees, April 2011.

U.S. Department of Defense Manual 8570.01-M, *Information Assurance Workforce Improvement Program,* Washington, D.C., December 19, 2005, incorporating change 3, January 24, 2012.

U.S. Government Accountability Office, *Cybersecurity Human Capital: Initiatives Need Better Planning and Coordination,* GAO-12-8, November 29, 2011.

Wheeler, Christopher H., "Search, Sorting, and Urban Aglomeration," *Journal of Labor Economics,* Vol. 19, No. 4, October 2001, pp. 879–899.

White House, "The Comprehensive National Cybersecurity Initiative," web page, undated. As of April 29, 2014: http://www.whitehouse.gov/issues/foreign-policy/cybersecurity/national-initiative

Yang, Yubao, and Rahul Telang, "Effectiveness of Software Assurance Programs: Evidence from Common Criteria," INFORMS annual meeting, Washington, D.C., October 2008.

Zweben, Stuart, and Betsy Bizot, "2012 Taulbee Survey," *Computing Research News,* May 2013, pp. 11–60.